THE WHIRLWIND

John L. Bullis and his Seminole-Negro Scouts

Grady E. McCright

Copyright © 2012 Grady E. McCright

All rights reserved.

ISBN: 1492729833
ISBN-13: 978-1492729839

THE WHIRLWIND

A portion of this work was published in the True West issue of October 1981.

DEDICATION

For our younger grandchildren: Zackary, Rion, Peyton, Aidan, Evan, Chandler, Garrett, Maddy, and Caleb

--And—

To the Foot Soldier who also fought in the West

CONTENTS

	Acknowledgments	vii
	Preface	1
1	Civil War Aftermath	4
2	Indian Turmoil	9
3	Texas' Plight	15
4	Indian Scrapper	19
5	Seminole—Negro Scouts	34
6	Engagements	50
7	Eighty Days on an Apache Trail	60
8	Last Battle	75
9	Bullis Leaves Texas	83
	Footnotes	102
	Bibliography	113

ACKNOWLEDGMENTS

Works of history are seldom written without the assistance of countless contributors. To everyone who helped, both knowingly and unknowingly, go my deepest thanks. Those listed below deserve a special acknowledgment

First and foremost, my thanks to the National Archives for opening their massive files and for locating and supplying photographs used to illustrate this work. Without the assistance of the Archive staff this story could not have been told.

I am grateful to James Fenton who made available his collection of materials on John L. Bullis and answered numerous questions which saved many hours of poring through ancient documents. He also provided several leads on the location of additional sources.

My appreciation is extended to both Phillis Dillard and the staff of New Mexico State University Library and to Pat Greathouse and the staff of Thomas Branigan Memorial Library, both in Las Cruces, New Mexico for giving invaluable research assistance and for obtaining research material through interlibrary loads.

I wish to acknowledge the photograph research conducted by Judy Ranney and the personnel at the Institute of Texas Cultures. At a critical time in rounding up illustrations, they came through with needed photographs and obtained permission for their use.

Thank you, Vera Bullis who took of her time to answer an inquiry that resulted in new sources and additional information.

Paul McCright and James Powell read and provided valuable comment on parts of this manuscript, and without their critique and suggestions it might have never been published. Hopefully, only they know how badly their help was needed.

To my friend, Beth Mahill, of Mayhill, New Mexico, who provided information on Bullis Spring which is the former Salvation Spring in Bullis' journal. This spring is on land in the Guadalupe Mountains in southeastern New Mexico once owned by her Great Grandfather, Cliborne Gentry Prude.

It is with all admiration that I recognize the valuable aid provided by the Internet. This amazing collection of knowledge is a wonderful research tool.

And to my friend Shane Jahn who provided photographs of the Bullis Gap area and helped me describe the country.

To my wife, Marie, who read and edited all of it, again and again. I am grateful for unselfishly giving of her time that this document might be written.

PREFACE

In mid-winter of 1878-79, a small party of Apache braves drifted south from the Mescalero Reservation in New Mexico Territory. They traveled along the Pecos River to a point near its junction with the Rio Grande. Here, in Texas, the warriors plundered isolated villages and ranches taking horses, cattle, and various other spoils.

A few weeks later, in late January, Lieutenant John Lapham Bullis, Commander of the Seminole - Negro scouts stationed at Fort Clark, Texas about 30 miles from Del Rio, was ordered to pursue the marauders whenever and wherever they could be located and return them to the fort to answer for their atrocities.

Once Bullis' scouts caught the Apaches' scent, there was no shaking him and his detachment. The command endured cold, wind, snow, range fire, and even rattlesnakes in their relentless stalk.

They suffered from lack of water, insufficient food, worn out horses and underfed stock as well as overwork and exhaustion; yet, the detail stuck to the trail like glue.

The campaign ended with Bullis' return to Fort Clark after traveling 1266 miles astride a horse and spending eighty nights under the stars. This was one of the longest small force scouting ventures on record, and it was conducted across some of the Southwest's most desolate and forbidding country.

Upon his return, Bullis, who has been called "The most successful Indian fighter in the history of the American Army," filed a lengthy report on the expedition, and it is through his words that the true hardships necessary to win the West are revealed.

This is Bullis' story. His childhood and involvement in the War Between the States are briefly discussed, but this work is centered on Bullis' contribution to the expansion and settlement of the frontier. He spent most of his working life dealing with the wild tribes of Indians who made the opening of the West very bloody for the newcomers from the East.

Bullis' role in the post Civil War era was the protection of settlers and their families from the hazards of life at the edge of civilization.

A major contribution to the settlement of the frontier was made by Bullis and his Seminole-Negro Indian scouts. Never numbering more than 42, these scouts earned four Medals of Honor and fought in most of the larger Indian campaigns in West Texas during the decade of the 1870's.

Runaway slaves and their descendants intermarried with Seminole Indians in Florida, they were relocated to Indian Territory along with the Seminoles in early 1840's after some seven years of fighting with United States troops. One of their leaders, Wild Cat, organized an escape from this unhappy reservation life, and in 1850, many of the captives made a mad-dash for Mexico. They successfully crossed the border and established a village in Northern Mexico.

Here they stayed for some twenty years; however, growing disenchantment with the Mexican government caused them to seek asylum back in the United States, after the Civil War had been settled and slavery was no longer an issue. The first Seminole-Negroes arrived north of the border in 1870 and became Indian scouts for the Army.

Bullis served in the Union Army during the War of the Rebellion but was discharged when the conflict ended. Deciding that Army life suited his nature, he was re-commissioned and wound up on the Texas border with Mexico for the duration of the Indian fighting in that state. He soon became the trusted leader of the detachment of Seminole-Negro scouts. It was, perhaps, his most successful assignment in the military, and the harsh duty seemed to agree with his disposition very well.

He later became a military Indian Agent and managed several reservations in New Mexico and Arizona Territories.

In January 1897, he was promoted to the rank of Major and became the U. S. Army Paymaster. When he retired at mandatory age, he was promoted to Brigadier General and he and his family returned to his adopted home state and settled in a now peaceful San Antonio.

General Bullis was beloved by the citizens of Texas for his frontier actions on their behalf. His story should be told. He was one of the great U. S. Army scouts during the Indian Wars, and his exploits deserve to live on in the hearts and minds of today's people.

Texans owe a great deal to Bullis and his Seminole-Negro Indian scouts. Bullis and his scouting command spent more than 40 years serving with the United States Army in a very harsh and hostile environment, constantly in danger from the hostiles for at least ten of those years. These scouts saved the lives of many white settlers and finally were involved in putting to rest the last Indian attacks in the State. Although the hostile depredations waxed and waned over the post-Civil War period, they did not come to an end until 1881.

1 CIVIL WAR AFTERMATH

During the Civil War, the Western Indians crept back into control of the frontier. Most of the able-bodied civilians and almost the entire Army were back East fighting the war. This unique event in the early history of the Western United States allowed the Indians, who had been pushed back for many years by the advancement of the white man, the opportunity to retake the frontier.

The end of the War Between the States spelled the approaching end to the wild Indians of this Country. When the civilians and the Army returned to the frontier in large numbers, the Indians faced a greater threat to their way of life than they had experienced before war broke out.

Returning survivors of the Civil War were a hardened and restless lot. Those in the South returned to a worn out and decimated land with little prospect for economic growth. Many found their former homes destroyed, taken over by interlopers, re-possessed by the bank or abandoned. Many of the pre-war families were separated, dead, or misplaced. It was a desolate time for the losers of the conflict and many of the toughened men chose to drift west, sometimes with their women and sometimes alone.

These pioneers in the western movement had learned to fight

during the four years of war but they faced a bitter and violent native in the American Indian on whose land they squatted. They established large ranches by rounding up maverick cattle sporting no brand and attempted to establish and develop the small villages that soon began to spring up around the water sources and rivers. Others settled on land that could be farmed that could be irrigated by streams or rivers. Others just drifted from job to job, sometimes on the right side of the law and sometimes not.

Out of necessity during the war, firearms had progressed from cap and ball to cartridge munitions and repeating arms were just beginning to signal their impact by the end of conflict, and the Indians quickly recognized the need to cast off their ancient weapons and acquire more modern arms. The truth is that for six or eight years after the war, the natives rapidly became better armed than the soldiers who still carried their cap and ball weapons. In 1873, the Springfield model 1873, .45 caliber "Trap Door" was adopted by the Army but by that time, the Indians had in large measure stolen enough lever-action Winchesters to still be better equipped than the army with its single-shot "Trap Doors."

Rapid westward expansion was just around the corner, but before this could really get underway, the Indian problem had to be settled, or at least minimized. The Army re-established its western forts deemed necessary for protection against the Indian when the population began to push westward. The increased pressure on the Indians caused them to fight back with swelling vengeance, forcing the military to enlarge its effort to stamp out the threat to increasing numbers of settlers.

Families, schools, churches, merchants, farms, ranches, and railroads were necessary for America's expansion, and over the next few years, expand they did, not however, without a high cost in human suffering and death.

Rounding up and herding the Indians to areas set aside as

reservations seemed to these early-day politicians and policy makers as the most humane solution to a dreadful situation. Over the next decade or so, thousands of Native Americans were tricked, captured, or lulled into accepting the terms of peace and shuffled off or otherwise transported to the Government's idea of the perfect culmination of the problem.

There were, however, some independent souls among the tribes. These warriors just could not seem to tolerate the idea of giving up their birthright--their land and freedom. These mostly small bands would, from time-to-time, leave the reservation to rob, murder, and plunder. Oftentimes the warriors would simply slip back onto reservation lands and, for a time, go on living peacefully like the others. These activities went on for years and years.

In dealing with these small groups, the Army miserably expended more time, energy, and manpower than when the large tribes were on the loose because the small bands could and did move rapidly and they were harder to locate. Dealing with these small raiding parties proved extremely difficult for the military. The Indians would ride a fast little mustang to death, kill and eat it, and steal another. The Army rode slow, shod thoroughbred stock that required grain to maintain its stamina. In short, the Indians covered more miles in a day and the military could not keep up.

Were the free-roaming Apaches of the 1800's tough? There has not since been a clan residing in the United States that was as wiry, cunning, held the endurance, or had the knowledge of nature and how to live off the land as did the Apaches before they were confined to reservations. Martine and Kayihtah, Army scouts who led Lieutenant Gatewood to Geronimo in September 1886, reportedly once journeyed 135 miles on foot in 60 hours to deliver a message. But people adapt quickly once exposed to the soft life. In 1979, George Martine, son of Scout Martine, told this author that he and Kayihtah's son found themselves about 130 miles from Mescalero in the 1920's. They decided that if their fathers could do it so could they. The two boys started walking, trotting, and running home. George laughed and said that within 20 miles of starting the journey, they gave up and began hitchhiking.

Lt. John L. Bullis during his time on the Texas frontier. (Courtesy Legends of America)

2 INDIAN TURMOIL

During the last days of the Southwest Indian Campaigns, the Army expended thousands of horses, horseshoes, boot soles, and men in an attempt to keep the elusive Apache on his reservation. More often than not, after days, weeks, or even months in the wake of a small raiding party, the troops would return wearily to their fort, having never even caught sight of the hostiles. It seems that the Army details were always a few hours or days behind the warriors.

Requiring almost no support, a raiding party traveled light. The Army needed wagons and pack animals loaded down with supplies if the column was to be on the trail for more than a day or so. As a result, the braves moved faster, poisoned water holes and generally made life miserable for the troops.

The hardships endured by the soldier were much worse than the combat he engaged in with the Indian. He withstood drought, extreme heat and cold, hunger, cactus thorns, snakes, and last but not least, boredom. One of the longest scouting trips on record occurred in the winter and spring of 1879. This detail covered 1266 miles and required eighty days in the saddle. During this entire journey, only the advance party, made up of a couple of scouts, seized a glimpse of the Indians and then only one time. By the time the column re-grouped and moved forward, the war party had disappeared. This foray is a dynamic example of the difficulties involved in chasing the Apache over his home turf. The Indian knew the land and he knew how to move across it rapidly, quietly, and without leaving more than a mere trace of his passage.

When the victorious U. S. Army returned to the frontier at the close of the Civil War, they found the entire Southwest terrorized by the Apache. Having had their hands full dealing with Johnny Reb, the Federal Government had recalled nearly all of the soldiers formerly stationed in the West. The Apache had seized this opportunity and had raided, looted, killed, and retaken his Southwestern homeland.

After Appomattox, the Army was immediately returned to the frontier to restore peace and open the West for expansion. It was soon evident that the military tactics learned in four years of combat with the Confederacy would not work in subduing the Apache. The Army did not encounter large bodies of Indians standing in long skirmish lines. Instead, they discovered the hostiles to be hit-and-run guerrilla raiders. Expertly mounted, moving in small, fierce, swift-striking bands, the warriors were full of trickery and treachery, spreading fear wherever they went. The braves were fighting in the only way they knew, and it was effective.

When pursued, the Apache might do anything. A favorite trick of a raiding party was to split into smaller and smaller groups. Finally, the Army would be following only one or two of the larger group that had committed the atrocity. The only other option the military had was to follow suit and split itself into smaller and smaller groups to chase the entire dissolving band of raiders. This would lead to ambushes. The soldiers' best protection from death and injury was safety in numbers.

After splitting into small parties, a few braves would lead the trailing Army far away from the main body of hostiles which quickly regrouped. The Indians rode their horses until one gave out from exhaustion. It was quickly dispatched, a hind quarter cut off, and a meal prepared.

Another mount was stolen, and the party was once again underway. The Army, on the other hand, traveled in large columns on grain-fed animals towing pack trains carrying the supplies necessary to keep the large force moving. When their horses became tired, the military halted to feed and rest. It was a strange and frustrating experience for the soldiers. They seemed to almost never lay their eyes on the elusive Apache, let alone get their hands on them, unless they were themselves the hunted when the renegades lured the military into country favorable to the native such as waterless tracts or steep slopes ripe for rock slides.

Another ploy was to lead the entire column into ambush. The native knew the country; whereas, many times the soldier was the stranger. Dead-end canyons with only a narrow escape route, bottle-necked arroyos, and rugged, rocky terrain with narrow eyebrow trails were dangerous spots for the advancing Army.

Leading the troops across vast expanses of dry desert also served the Apaches well. The Indians knew where natural water might be found or they would strategically bury caches of food and water, and often stash fresh horses before starting the raid. The Army was at the mercy of the elements with both men and animals suffering terribly.

These experiences hunting the Indian soon caused the military commanders to consider employing local woodsmen and Native Americans to be their guides. Out of this idea was born the Indian scout. Members from various tribes were hired to be Army scouts. These were hard men who had lived in the frontier their entire lives and knew the ways of the pursued bands. They also knew the land. Since they were Indians, they thought like Indians and were wary of leading the Army into ambush. They could warn the officers before embarking across deserts that lacked watering holes. Even if caught unaware, these native trackers were much better at locating sources of grass and water than the eastern raised soldiers. In defense of the white man, it did not take him long to begin to understand the Indians and there were many white men who became famous for their ability to guide the Army in pursuit of the American Indian war parties. John Lapham Bullis became one of the best and, by all rights, should have become a famous historical figure.

Trouble between the white man and the Indian usually started when the pale face encroached on tribal land. The Indian retaliated and blood was shed. It is easy to understand both sides of the conflict since the Indian had possession of the Southwest for thousands of years before the white eyes even landed in the New World. The red man naturally resented his ancestral homeland being gobbled up by the latecomers. Conversely, the frontiersman saw the Indian as a savage who stood in the way of progress; he must be removed; by annihilation if necessary.

A Congressional Act ratified on June 30, 1834, defined as Indian country all of the land west of the Mississippi River not within the States of Louisiana, Missouri, or the Territory of Arkansas. It also authorized the President to keep the peace in this vast expanse by the use of military might, if required.[1]

In December of 1835, President Andrew Jackson pledged to the Indians that this land would be forever theirs.[2] Of course, this proved to be only a temporary commitment. The white man had an inherent zest for exploration, and he was not long in moving west of the Mississippi. By the fall of 1868, the Indian wars were at full tilt.

After the end of the War Between the States, the Army strength dwindled to a very small force. With the Indian troubles, this small number could not protect the settlers in the big country; so on July 28, 1866, the Army received the authority from Congress to increase its size to 55,000 men,[3]   But by 1874, due primarily to budget cuts, the staff had again been reduced to a mere 25,000 soldiers.[4] It remained at about this strength for twenty-five years.

If trouble started in the Southwest, troops had to be transferred from the Pacific or elsewhere, which left that section of the country undermanned. The Texas-Mexico border alone is 1500 miles long and was protected by only scattered military outposts. As one Texas Congressman declared, "The bones of more than forty passengers and stage drivers have been bleaching in the sun and crying aloud to Heaven that these savage warriors and Mexican robbers should be driven from our borders."[5]

On June 12, 1869, the Army received orders to pursue any Indians found not on reservation lands. They could treat the escapees in any manner that was deemed fit for the occasion.[6] It was left to the whim of the detail commander to decide whether the wanderers should be treated as friendly or hostile. The military did not, however, have the authority to enter reservations in pursuit of hostiles. These lands fell under the jurisdiction of the Department of the Interior, not the War Department. Therefore, raiding parties continued their hostile acts until surprised by an Army detail. They then hot-footed it back inside the boundaries of their Agency.

The resident Indian Agent was understandably reluctant to admit that any of his wards had been involved in hostile acts. For several years, the War Department petitioned Congress to give the military authority over the reservations instead of the Department of the Interior. The Indian Agent would not turn over the hostiles even if he did know which braves were involved. To do so would have given the War Department added fodder to convince Congress that neither civilian agents nor the Department of the Interior could handle the Indian.

The Army was finally given authority to enter certain reservations in pursuit of hostiles on July 21, 1874. This action certainly gave the military a helping hand, but once on the reservation, the hostiles would melt into the mainstream of reservation life. It was like looking for a needle in a haystack. Which braves were the guilty ones?

Sergeant F. W. Klopper, Troop H, 4th Cavalry and group of Mescalero Apache Scouts, Fort Stanton, New Mexico in 1885. (Courtesy National Archives: U.S. Signal Corps Photo)

3 TEXAS' PLIGHT

By the late 1870's the large tribes had been successfully contained on various reservations in the Southwest. The main problem now was the small bands of renegade Mescalero Apaches who from time-to-time abandoned their reservation in south-central New Mexico Territory near the present-day town of Ruidoso. The reservation, located along the Tularosa River, is several hundred square miles of the most beautiful and remote lands in New Mexico. With groups of Indian families scattered all over this vast Agency, it was nearly impossible to locate the raiding party after they returned to the reservation and mixed back into the population.

Mescalero hunting parties would slip away from the Agency, and in a matter of a few days, they would penetrate deep into Texas to loot and kill. These small bands would move swiftly from place to place spreading death and destruction all across their backtrail. After some time in the area, they would break off the attacks and high-tail it back to the safety of Rio Tularosa.

A report to the Governor of Texas, O. M. Roberts, noted that the following depredations by hostile Indian bands had occurred in the state between 1865 and December 31, 1879:[7]

407 persons killed (including 13 Texas Rangers)

76 persons wounded (including 17 Rangers)

81 persons reported captured by Indians

20,521 horses and mules stolen by Indians

43,392 cattle stolen

2.430 sheep and goats stolen

The same report states that 123 bands of Indians were known to have entered Texas between May 1870 and the report date of December 31, 1879. The Texas Rangers alone had pursued 97 raiding parties since May 1874. The Rangers had, however, engaged in only 26 fights with the Redskins since May 1870. At least 77 Indians had been killed, 29 wounded, and 3 captured. The State had recovered 6,871 head of stock since August of 1870.

It is impossible to deny that the State of Texas was plagued by Indian renegade raiding parties. It is not possible, however, to identify how many of these bands came from the Mescalero Reservation in New Mexico Territory; yet it is a safe assumption that a sizable number did.

When renegades were in the area, their progress could be tracked by the incoming reports of depredations and murders. The following accounts are the slayings attributed to Indians during the month of April 1878. No doubt all of these killings were not the work of one raiding party as the locations are too widely separated for that, but they do indicate the seriousness of the raids on the Texas frontier.

On April 15, it was reported that Mescalero Apaches had stolen twelve mules near Fort Davis, Texas, a few days before. This same raiding party killed a mail rider on or about the 9th near the Escondido Station. After six days trailing the band, the mail was recovered but no Indians were captured.

The first Fort Davis was established in the fall of 1854 and ironically was named for the Secretary of War, Jefferson Davis by the United States military. This fort was for the protection of travelers on the San Antonio--El Paso (then called Franklin) road. In the fall of 1855, Lieutenant Zenas R. Bliss arrived at the fort after a seventeen day stage trip from San Antonio. He later wrote, "The post was the most beautifully situated of any that I have ever seen. It was in a narrow canyon with perpendicular sides, the walls of which were about 200 feet in height." Bliss also noted that camp life was very dull and there was not a house within one-hundred miles. Although he acknowledged that game was plentiful, he noted that, "The Indians were so bad that no one ever thought of going more than three or four miles from the Post."

In an attempt to conquer the lack of water in the desert west of the Fort, in 1856 seventy-four camels were brought to the post from the Middle East. Other camels were delivered in 1859 and 1860 but the experiment proved a limited success, the entire idea was forgotten with the onset of the Civil War and was never repeated. It is reported that stray camels would occasionally be seen in the west Texas area for years after the experiment was discarded.

When Federal troops abandoned the Fort in 1862, it lay in ruin until 1867 when it was again occupied; however, the location was moved to a flat area east of the canyon where the first fort was located. By virtue of its higher elevation, Davis had the most favorable climate of any fort in the state yet it was finally decommissioned in 1891.

The following persons were all reported killed on the same day, April 17, 1878: W. M. McCall, nine miles from Fort Quitman; Frederick B. Moore, at San Ygnacio; Vicenti Robledo, Brown's Ranch; and George and Dick Taylor, Steele's Ranch on the Nueces River.

Guadaloupe Basan was killed at Rancho Soledad on the 18th. Nearby, a Mexican and his wife were killed, tied together, and thrown over a horse. Also, John Jordan was slain at Charco Escondido. All of these deaths occurred in Duval County.

The 19th brought death to Margarito Rodriguez and Jose Maria Canales. Canales was shot near Quijotes Gordes and thrown into a campfire that consumed his lower extremities.

On the 20th, Lonjinio Gonzales, a mail rider, was murdered at Point of Rocks, 18 miles from Fort Davis. Mescalero Apaches from the New Mexico Reservation reportedly took the lives of two unidentified men on this same date.[8]

The Indian problem in Texas became so grave that in 1879, Governor Roberts requested the military to provide a small detail of soldiers to accompany a surveying party in the Texas panhandle as protection against Indian attack.[9]

This survey party was to establish 3,000,000 acres which would be offered to anyone willing to build the State a new capitol in Austin. Since the State Treasury was not financially capable of producing the necessary funds, the people decided to swap some of Texas' large land holdings for a state house.

Several successful businessmen from the Chicago area took Texas up on the deal and they constructed the beautiful Capitol which is still used today. The three million acres became the world's largest ranch, the famed XIT. This cattle empire operated until it was sold off in 1912.[10]

4 INDIAN SCRAPPER

The Indian Wars produced extraordinary men. One such man was Captain Albert H. Pfeiffer, a Dutchman in the New Mexico Volunteers, stationed at Fort McRae. While on a family outing with his Spanish wife, her two maids, and a detail of six soldiers, Pfeiffer was swimming in the Rio Grande some distance from the Fort when he was interrupted by a band of Apaches. As the Indians closed in on the small group, the soldier escort was killed to the man, and the three women taken prisoner. The renegades then went after the Captain who, upon hearing the shots, climbed from the water and armed himself with his rifle. Naked and wet, he started firing and retreating toward the Fort. Several hours went by in a shoot-and-run fight as Pfeiffer slowly made his way to safety. By the time he reached the Fort, his body was badly sunburned and he had an arrow through his back which had penetrated so deeply that the point could be seen sticking out of his stomach.

Troops were sent out to pursue the Indians who abandoned their captives when the detail stormed from the Fort. Mrs. Pfeiffer and one attendant were killed and another was severely wounded.

This tragic event left the Captain with a keen hatred for the Redskin and he devoted his life to killing Indians. Whenever possible, Pfeiffer went out alone to hunt. He claimed that a pack of wolves always followed, knowing that there would be dead Indians along his backtrail.

Pfeiffer continued on the frontier for many years, eventually being promoted to Colonel. In January 1864, he was with Colonel Kit Carson when they forced the surrender of eight thousand Navajos in their twenty-seven mile long stronghold, Canyon de Chelly. Carson penetrated the canyon at one end while Pfeiffer's hard fighting command blocked the Navajos' retreat at the other.[11]

Lieutenant John Lapham Bullis of the 24th Infantry was another outstanding Indian campaigner; yet, unlike Pfeiffer, he hoarded no hatred for the redman. He simply had a job to do and he set about it with gusto. While Bullis was the Chief Scout at Fort Clark, Texas, he engaged in some of the most exciting and least known battles in the annals of American history. Recorded descriptions of his actions and physical appearance conjure the classic frontier scout who knew as much about the habits of the Indian as the Indian himself.

Bullis was a small, wiry man who sported a black mustache on a face burned as red as his adversary, the Apache.[12] He was a tireless marcher who drove his command hard; nevertheless, he was loved by his Seminole scouts, one and all.

Frederic Remington said that Bullis was a man who must surely pay high life insurance premiums as he seemed to have a knack for locating hostiles and taking them on when his forces were out numbered many fold. The Lieutenant was a successful commander who never lost one of his scouts through eight combat-locked years with the Comanches, Mescaleros, Kickapoos, and Lipans.[13]

When on the trail, Bullis was said to remove only one tin from the pack each day; be it peaches or beans, he would make it do. Oftentimes he lived off the land, as did his scouts. They survived on rabbit, rattlesnake, or venison.[14]

Once as they made an early morning raid on a temporary Indian camp, the hostiles scattered just as the troops arrived, leaving fresh horse meat roasting over the open fire. Bullis and his scouts, who had not had breakfast, abandoned the chase and feasted on the captured vittles.[15]

The Lieutenant moved with such speed that he became known by both the hostile Indians and his scouts as "The Whirlwind." He was also affectionately referred to as "Thunderbolt" by the Seminole scouts.[16]

Frederic Remington noted how close white officers became to their black charges: Personal relations can be much closer between white officers and colored soldiers than in white regiments without breaking the barriers which are necessary to army discipline. The men look up to a good officer, rely on him in trouble, and even seek him for advice in their small personal affairs.

Bullis certainly fit the description Remington gave of the relationship between white officers and the black soldiers and this statement may, in fact, have been written about him since Remington had been on a scout with the 24th and knew Bullis in Arizona.

When a child was born to a scout, Bullis would ride out to their village, some three miles from Fort Clark, to wish the new arrival well. If the baby was a boy, "The Whirlwind" would lift him up and exclaim how he would make a fine scout someday. On at least one occasion, Bullis was asked to perform a marriage ceremony for one of his command. He officiated at the festivities with Bible in hand.[17]

The Lieutenant defended the scouts when they had trouble extracting payment for their services from the Federal Government, and when faced with disbandment, he fought for their rights. Bullis was also instrumental in gaining permission for the Seminole families to settle on Las Moras Creek. He was their friend, and the scouts as well as their descendants, remain loyal to the name of John L. Bullis even to this day.

The Seminole's feelings for Bullis are best summed up in a statement made years later by a former scout, Joseph Phillips:

> The scouts thought a lot of Bullis. Lieutenant Bullis was the only officer ever did stay the longest with us. That fella suffer jest like we all did out in de woods. He was a good man. He was a Injun fighter. He was tuff. He didn't care how big a bunch dey wuz, he went into 'em everytime, but he look after his men. His men was on equality, too. He didn't stan' back and say "Go yonder"; he would say, "Come on, boys, let's go get 'em."[18]

Even today, descendants of the scouts meet annually at the Seminole cemetery, located near Bracketville, Texas on the third Saturday in September to honor their ancestors and in remembrance of their bygone leader, John L. Bullis.

Brigadier General D. S. Stanley stated that, "Bullis... has the most successful career of an Indian fighter that has ever been recorded in the history of the American Army."[19]

Lieutenant Colonel I. D. Davis described Bullis as, "...a most diligent and attentive officer, a strict disciplinarian, and a man of the best moral character I ever saw in the Army."[20]

A native of New York State, Bullis enrolled in the volunteer Army during the Civil War at Farmington on August 8, 1862, at the age of twenty-one. He was mustered into active service as a corporal with Company H, 126th New York Infantry on August 22, 1862. In September of that year, he took part in the battle at Harper's Ferry. The Spring of 1863 found him in a skirmish near Centerville, Virginia.

In July of 1863, Bullis had the misfortune to attend the battle of Gettysburg. He was captured by the Rebel forces and confined at Richmond, Virginia, until paroled on September 29. Bullis immediately made his way to Camp Parole, Maryland, where he reported for duty.

There he was granted a fifteen day furlough to wash out the cobwebs of the Confederate prison.

Shortly after his return to active duty, Bullis was offered the chance to accept an appointment as a Captain in the 118th United States Colored Infantry Volunteers. He accepted the challenge of being a white officer in a Negro regiment and was given his chance to command with Company A. This company, while under Bullis' command, endured almost continuous fire at Dutch Gap Canal, Virginia, for nearly three months during the winter of 1864 and 1865. He served with this company until honorably mustered out of service as a major on February 6, 1866, near Brownsville, Texas.[21]

John Lapham Bullis was born to Doctor Abram Rogers Bullis and Lydia Lapham on April 17, 1841, in their cobblestone house at Macedon, New York. The oldest of seven children, John grew up in rich farming country in the shadow of both sets of grandparents. Charles Bullis had migrated with his wife and John's father from Vermont some twenty years before. The maternal family, headed by John Lapham, can be traced back to the 1600's through Rhode Island to England.

Young Bullis attended Macedon Academy four miles from his home, and later his education was broadened at the neighboring village of Lima. Always athletic and on the lookout for adventure, he engaged in the typical winter activities of the cold Northeast, and in the lush summers, the youngster worked on the farms of his grandparents. The boy's love for the outdoors and the ways of nature are evident from his earliest years. Fishing, hunting, and trapping were among his favorite pastimes. It is said that as a teenager, he ran a trap-line as far away as Canada.

Bullis' family were Quakers and they regularly attended the meetings; nevertheless, the non-violent teachings did not take with young Bullis. His entire adult life was spent seeking employment where physical force was necessary. He did, however, reveal that he held an understanding of the Quaker beliefs in a letter to his mother written while on parole from the Confederate prison:

> I am keeping a Rebel from fighting now I
> suppose, although I am doing nothing and
> the Rebel the same. Rather Quaker warfare, I
> think.[22]

After leaving the military in South Texas, Bullis drifted to the Mississippi River and obtained employment supplying firewood to the steamboats. He stockpiled wood at several points along the river, particularly St. Francis, Mississippi and Helena, Arkansas. From these warehouses, the woodcutter met arriving steamers and sold what fuel he could. This was a backbreaking business not suited to an adventurer, so he soon sought other opportunities.[23]

Having tasted military life, Bullis found it to his liking. Therefore, when the Army began its buildup to combat the Indian threat in the Southwest, Bullis made himself available. He was granted an appointment as Second Lieutenant in the 41st Infantry on September 3, 1867.[24]

Bullis joined the 41st in Brownsville, Texas where the unit was garrisoned at Fort Brown and ordered to protect the mouth of the Rio Grande. Detachments of the unit were stationed along the Rio Grande to protect the fords and other strategic locations. Brownsville had been an important port for the Confederates during the War Between the States and had been a bustle of activity until the Union took procession of the town in November 1863. The fort was almost completely destroyed by the retreating Confederate soldiers so one of the first tasks of the 41st was rebuilding the facility.

It should be noted that this early time in the Reconstruction Period in Texas was not met with a great deal of friendship by the local residents. The U.S, Army occupation was not well received and the presence of black soldiers was viewed by the Texans with even more distaste. It was not a pleasant time for the occupation troops or the local residents. Relations were shaky to say the least. It is difficult to know if Bullis and his brother officers spent more of their time managing the 41st or dealing with unhappy Texans.

In October 1867, a large hurricane crossed the shoreline near Brownsville and completely destroyed the 41st outpost on the island of Brazos Santiago. The post was flooded and four troopers drowned. The town of Brownsville was also damaged and flooded. At Fort Brown, sixteen newly constructed buildings were flattened.

In March, 1868, the 41st received orders to relocate westward and occupy several posts along the upper Rio Grande. While the country was harsh, the relations with locals improved somewhat by moving to the western part of Texas.

The 41st occupied Forts McIntosh, Duncan, and Clark. Headquarters along with Bullis were posted at Fort Clark near Del Rio. Shortly, garrisons of the 41st occupied Forts Stockton, Inge, Davis, McKavett, Concho, and Quitman. They were engaged in protecting the entire western part of Texas from the Mexican border to the Staked Plains. Their mission included garrison duties such as fatigue, guard, and construction; installation of telegraph lines, protection of mail and stage routes, road repair, and protection of the few settlers in the vast area from Indians and bandit attacks.

In 1869, the 41st and 38th Infantry were combined into the 24th U.S. Infantry. All three of these units were made up of Negro soldiers and white officers. During the War of the Rebellion, Confederate authorities had threatened to execute any white officer captured while in command of Negro troops. Because of this and other hardships endured by these white officers, the United States Congress had given preference to those officers who had served with colored soldiers in the War. Again Bullis accepted the challenge and was transferred to the 24th.

The Army in the Southwest contained two cavalry units, the 9th and 10th, and two Infantry units, the 24th and the 25th, that were made up entirely of black soldiers. These troops served the United States well.

While the cavalry units took to the field and made long scouts, the infantry units performed garrison duties most of the time or manned sub-posts, or strung telegraph wire and maintained roads. Detachments at the sub-posts were rotated every 30-days back to the Fort and other troops replaced them on sub-post duty.

This is not to say that the infantry was always on foot. Certain elements of infantry were mounted from time to time and supported the cavalry on scouting expeditions.

Texas service for the newly created black units began in August 1870 and lasted for more than ten years. The Twenty-Fourth was headquartered near Fort McKavett and had detachments stationed at Forts Bliss, Clark, Davis, Duncan, Quitman, and Stockton. Bullis was assigned to Fort Clark, at Brackettville and near Del Rio.

Fort McKavett was perched atop a high bluff above the San Saba River in Menard County. It was established in 1852 to protect the Texas frontier. After the Indian War in Texas was over, it was abandoned in 1883.

These black troops served the United States well. History, to date, has not seen fit to bestow upon these Negro soldiers their earned credit in the Indian Campaigns. Many accounts of the battles fought by the black man mention the units involved but do not point out that these horsesoldiers and footsoldiers were indeed Negroes. They did have white officers, but the man who did the fighting and the dying was the same man who just a few short years before had been a slave to the whites. Now he was making a gigantic contribution to the opening of the West for the white man's exploitation.

Black soldiers became known by the Indians as Buffalo Soldiers because their kinky hair resembled the hair on top of the great bison's head. The Indians learned to respect the Negro soldier's fighting ability after a few confrontations, and the troopers were proud of the handle given them by their adversaries. The 10th Calvary even adopted the buffalo as the central figure in its coat of arms.[25]

One person who left a written record that testified to the fighting abilities of the black soldier was General Custer's wife, Libby. Telling of a skirmish with the Chief Roman Nose and the Cheyenne that occurred at Fort Wallace, Kansas in 1867, she wrote:

> ... While the fight was going on, the two officers in command found themselves near each other on the skirmish line, and observed a wagon with four mules tearing out to the line of battle. It was filled with Negroes [sic], standing up, all firing in the direction of the Indians. The driver lashed the mules with his black snake, and roared at them as they ran. When the skirmish line was reached, the colored men leaped out and began firing again. No one had ordered them to leave their picket-station, but they were determined that no soldiering should be carried on in which their valor was not proved.

Although much recorded history focuses on the fighting that occurred between the buffalo soldiers and the Indians, in reality, most of the military's time was spent in monotony and boredom brought about by the remoteness of their forts and encampments. Most of these posts were isolated from civilization and the few that were close to settlements, found little social life catering to black soldiers.

Since the cavalry frequently left the outposts to perform patrol missions, most of the garrison duties fell to the infantry. The mounted cavalry was better suited to engage the rapidly deploying western tribes. Because mounted soldiers were in the field more and covered more country, they encountered the raiding parties more often than the infantry. Consequently, much more historical ink is devoted to the cavalry than the infantry.

The infantrymen constructed, maintained, and guarded the posts; provided escort duty for paymasters, supply trains, and oftentimes, railroad construction crews. They guarded waterholes and stagecoach relay stations; cut, transported, and installed telegraph poles, and strung wire. This was hot, dirty, unglamorous, and monotonous labor, but it was vitally important to the settling of the West.

Another grueling task that fell to the infantry was the building of roads across the frontier. Many of the popular roads of today had their start from dirt, two-track wagon trail scrapped clear of large boulders, cactus, and mesquite by the black soldier of the late 1800's. Company B of the twenty-fourth was assigned the responsibility of building a road from San Felipe to Fort Davis. The assignment lasted from September 1879 until January 1880.

The black infantry soldier seems to have been better suited to his toil than his white counterpart. Only recently freed from slavery, the black soldiers had the lowest desertion rate in the military, tallied sick call, and demonstrated much fewer alcohol problems than similar white units.

Grand housing conditions did not reward the frontier enlisted man for his long hours, monotony, and drudgery as reported by Colonel Edmound Shriver who in 1872 described the conditions at Fort Clark, which was considered one of the better posts:

> The quarters are wretchedly [constructed] and therefore nothing beyond shelter and ordinary police can reasonably be looked for. All except two companies of

> cavalry are in huts . . . the regimental
> Adjutant's office is in a tent . . . the
> laundresses living in miserable shanties . . .
> the public stores are imperfectly covered
> with paulins [canvas tarps] or put in insecure
> huts . . .

Life on the frontier was not a comfortable, nor by our current standards, a pleasant experience; nevertheless, to the black soldier it was a far cry above slave conditions that most of them had known and at least they were freedmen.

One of the sought after assignments for an infantryman was to be detailed to the mounted infantry in support of the cavalry or for scouting duties. Although somewhat more dangerous than post tasks, this stint provided a much needed interruption from the dreariness of garrison fatigue chores.

Bullis' first major fight with the redskins came on September 1, 1871. He and four privates from Company H, 9th Cavalry were traveling some distance from the main body of troops when they discovered three Indians driving a herd of three hundred stolen cattle. Bullis immediately ordered an attack. The Indians abandoned the herd and fled. The five soldiers pressed them hard for about a mile before the three were joined by fifteen additional braves. Upon reaching the top of a small hill, the renegades turned on Bullis and his men. The soldiers dismounted and attempted to take on all fifteen hostiles.

It was not long before the sound of gunfire brought ten more Indians into the skirmish. Bullis was now outnumbered by almost six to one. The five soldiers poured a steady fire into the entrenched Indians for over thirty minutes, but Bullis realized that it was impossible to dislodge the Indians without reinforcements and broke off the conflict

He was, however, able to grab another herd that the late arriving Indians had left to enter the fight. Bullis and his men recovered nearly 500 head of cattle on that day.[26]

 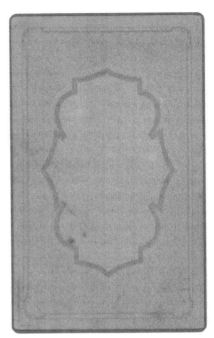

2nd Lt. John L. Bullis (Courtesy SMU Digital collections)

Post Headquarters, Fort Clark, Texas (Courtesy National Archives: Quartermaster General)

Barracks Interior, Fort Clark, Texas. (Courtesy National Archives: Quartermaster General)

5 SEMINOLE--NEGRO SCOUTS

Bullis became commander of the Fort Clark scouts in May 1873. It was as Chief Scout that John Bullis found his finest hour. Most of his service time while in this command was spent afield, and it was here that he learned to think like an Indian. Contact with hostiles occurred more frequently when on the trail as a small party rather than as a large Infantry column. Bullis and his scouts certainly found their share of hostiles.

The scouts of Fort Clark consisted mainly of Seminole-Negro Indians. These scouts were for the most part descendants of runaway slaves who had taken refuge among the Seminole Indians who themselves had fled into the swamps and the Everglades of Florida.

Over the years, the Negroes intermixed and intermarried with the Indians. They learned the language, the customs, and the crafts of their constant companions. About the only remaining influence of their slave ancestors was religion. The majority of Seminole-Negroes were still Baptists as their forefathers had been before the flight to the Seminoles. An unusual custom still practiced by descendants of these people is that for their communion services, they use tea to represent the blood of Jesus, not grape juice or wine.

The Seminoles and the black runaways had fought the American government in two Seminole Wars. The first war started in 1817 and the second in 1836. Each time the Indians retreated deeper into the Florida swamplands. Although, many of the combatants were captured and forced to relocate to Indian Territory, the remnants remained and still live in Florida today. They were never routed by Army troops although a treaty was finally signed that relocated the remainder to what is now Oklahoma.

John Horse was the leader of the Black Seminoles in the Second War. He was a fierce fighter and was well respected by U. S. forces. He was, however, a man of peace and, in 1837, he agreed to surrender terms and agreed to relocate to Indian Territory. By 1840, he was married to Susan July.

A runaway slave born about 1812, John Horse was living on his owner's place near Tampa Bay in 1826 but little is known of his earlier years. In later years, he was chief spokesman for the Seminole-Negroes and represented them well. He was loved and respected by the entire clan.

During this war, John Horse, Wild Cat, and Chief Osceola were captured by U. S. Troops and imprisoned at Fort Marion in St. Augustine. This event forged the close association between the two leaders that continued through adversity until wild Cat's death in 1857. The two men fasted while in prison until they could slip through the bars and make their escape. Osceola took ill and died, leaving the Seminole Nation in able leadership of Wild Cat.

The Seminole-Negro members of the tribe proved themselves able fighters in the Seminole Wars. General Philip Jessup stated in 1836 that "This is a Negro, not an Indian War." Jessup also declared that, "Throughout my operations I found the Negroes the most active and determined warriors . . ."

With slavery still legal in the Southern part of the United States, the Seminole-Negro members of the tribe remained on the reservation for fear of capture by white slavers. In fact, John Horse's sister, Juana lost two children to slavers and they were never recovered. The Black Seminoles lived a sedate life confined pretty much to the reservation property; however, discontent grew with each passing year. The blacks were mistreated by other tribes confined to reservations in the Territory.

Around 1850, the dissatisfaction became unbearable and several hundred Seminoles and Negroes left the United States and fled into Mexico under the leadership of Chief Wild Cat. In Mexico where slavery was illegal, they felt safe, and with the promise of employment by the Government and the assurance of land, a large group agreed to relocate.

Settling at Nacimiento in the state of Coahuila Mexico in the Santa Rosa Mountains, the tribe became farmers in the fertile valley along the Sabinas River. Already residents of the 26 square mile compound were other tribes of Indians such as the Creek, Biloxi, and Kickapoos. From all reports, the Seminole-Negroes mixed with this group and a restrained peace ensued for several years.

Some of the tribe signed up to serve the Mexican government as a defense force against roving war parties of both Comanches and Apaches. Throughout this frontier military activity, the Seminole-Negroes again proved their worth. It is likely that their scouting and sign reading skills in desert terrain was perfected during this time.

Chief Wild Cat was the leader of the Seminole group and Chief John Horse was the leader of the Black Seminole sect of the tribe. It was John Horse, also known as Juan Caballo, John Cowaya, and Gopher John, who became an officer in the Mexican Army and was the appointed leader of the scouting efforts for the Army. He remained the leader of the black Seminoles for nearly 50-years.

While in Mexico, the Seminole-Negroes became known as Mascogos. This name may have been derived from the Muskogee language spoken by the Seminoles. The tribe also spoke Hitchiti and after the move to Mexico, Spanish. The Black Seminoles also spoke a slave language similar to the African dialect known as Gullah. In Oklahoma the Blacks were known as Freedmen. In Texas, the group was often called Seminole with no reference to color.

Over the years, the Black Seminoles adapted dress from the Southeastern Indians. They wore brightly colored shirts, leggings with moccasins, and an abundance of silver jewelry. For their headdress, they adopted the cloth turbans with an occasional feather.

As time passed, tensions between the Mascogos, the Seminoles, and other tribes living on the land in the Santa Rosa Mountains began to build. Wild Cat died along with some 40 others in 1857 from an epidemic of smallpox. His passing certainly did not serve to quell the friction between the different ethnic groups. A rumor persists that Wild Cat was killed by John Horse but seems far fetched since he and John Horse had shared leadership for many years, the smallpox epidemic was running wild at the time of Wild Cat's death, and the fact that Wild Cat was held in high esteem by all the different peoples who lived in the area. Nevertheless, his death hastened the dissolution of the pact that held the various ethnic groups together.

By 1861, nearly all the Seminole had returned to Oklahoma. The Mascogos remained in Mexico but from that time on, the turbulence expanded. Hostile Indian attacks increased, there was conflict over land and cattle, and relations with the Mexican Government began to deteriorate rapidly. Part of the problems in Mexico seem to have been over religion. Mexico was and still is largely Roman Catholic while the Black Seminoles were Baptist. Since neither faith accepted the habits or beliefs of the other, conflict arose.

Within twenty years, the Seminoles' relationship with the Mexican government deteriorated to the point that they sought permission to return to the United States. It just so happened that the timing was excellent since the United States Army was still having a terrible time with the native tribes in the Southwest and had decided that it took an Indian to catch an Indian. Therefore, the Army was authorized to enlist Native American Scouts.

In 1870, Colonel Jacob De Gress, Commander at Fort Duncan sent an official invitation to the remaining people in Mexico to discuss terms for returning to the United States. Captain Frank Perry journeyed to Mexico to flesh out the terms. In the temporary absence of Chief John Horse, John Kibbetts represented the Mascogos. It was agreed that while they awaited an American decision about resettlement, the tribe would prepare to leave Nacimiento and journey to Fort Duncan.

They struck an agreement with the U. S. Army to return north of the border and serve as scouts against the troublesome Apaches who were still raiding in southwest Texas.

The Seminole-Negro scouts with their families arrived at Fort Duncan under the command of Chief John Horse. By formal treaty they had agreed to serve as scouts and were given permission to return north of the Rio Grande. For their service, they would receive pay as regular soldiers. After their enlistment period expired, they were to be given land grants in the States and allowed to remain as citizens. These land grants were never provided.

Fort Duncan was established in 1849 where Eagle Pass now stands on a site previously selected by Captain Robert E. Lee of the engineering corps. The village gained its name from the Rio Grande ford known by the Indians and Spaniards as "Pass of the Eagle" due to a large eagle's nest in a huge pecan tree where Rio Escondido empties into the Rio Grande.

Captain Sydney Burbank and his Companies A and F of the First Infantry arrived on March 27, 1849 to establish and occupy the fort. This group of soldiers had just created Fort Inge on the Leona River near present-day Uvalde. Brevet Lieutenant Colonel W. G. Freeman inspected the Fort in 1853 and wrote that "From information furnished to me I am inclined to think that a better site for the post than the present one would be some 30 miles below where the Presidio road crosses the Rio Grande." This is about the location of the present day town of Guerrero, Mexico. Nevertheless, present-day Eagle Pass, Texas and Piedras Negras, Mexico sprang up to supply the Fort with services. The Fort served the United States through the Mexican Revolution when 16,000 troops stationed there protected the U. S. border from Mexican invaders. After World War I, the Fort was left in the hands of a small caretaker force until sold to the City of Eagle Pass in 1938.

The scouting detachment was first organized at Fort Duncan by Major Zenas R. Bliss, 25th Infantry Regiment. The first muster-in roll of the Seminole-Negro Indian Scouts was authorized by the Commanding Officer of the Department of Texas, dated Headquarters, Department of Texas, Austin, Texas 20 July 1870. The enlistment was from August 16 for a term of six months unless sooner discharged. The pay was sixteen dollars per month. The following ten names are listed in the muster in rolls:

Name	Rank	Age	comments
Kibbitt, John	1st Sergeant	60	Deputy Chief to John Horse
Dixie, Joe	Private	19	
Factor, Dindie	Private	21	
Factor, Hardie	Private	60	
Factor, Pompie	Private	16	Medal of Honor
Fay, Adams	Private	18	
Kibbitt, Bobby	Private	20	
Thompson, John	Private	18	

| Ward, John | Private | 20 | Medal of Honor |
| Washington, George | Private | 21 | |

It is interesting to note that John Horse is absent from the roll. Although he led the scouts in their military activities in Mexico, he never became a member of the United States contingent of scouts. Instead he became the diplomat for the clan and spent his time trying to better the living conditions and ensure that families were adequately provided compensation for the scouts' service to the Country. He was nearing 60 years of age by the time the Mascogos left Mexico even though the first Muster Roll lists two scouts at age 60.

Eventually numbering just over 40, the Seminole scouts were provided with arms, ammunition, and rations by the military. They supplied their own mounts and clothes. The most common dress was a modified Indian costume augmented by some white man's duds. They were not fashion models for the Army, but they knew the scouting business well.

Archie Waters relates a story in the El Paso Times concerning a scout named Picayune John who told his young officer, probably John Bullis, that there were Indians all around their camp one night. The officer was reluctant to believe the scout but the scout persisted so the officer agreed to prepare for an attack. It seems that Picayune John heard the unlikely mimicking of a desert owl and was certain that the sound was made by hostiles. In the cool desert night, many small animals and some larger ones are on the move, but with a group of noisy men camped nearby, most of the animals stay silent so as not to alert the men. When Picayune John heard the owl sound, his keen ears knew it was man made, not owl made.

Just before dawn, John woke the officer and told him that the renegades were moving toward the camp. Soon the firing of the pickets could be heard and an intense fight ensued. The scouts were able to hold off the raiders until light when the marauders broke off the attack. The troops recovered a number of horses the Indians had abandoned when they fled.

Although Waters admits that some of the following is speculation, it clearly demonstrates the capability of a good scout and there is no doubt that Picayune John was a skilled tracker. John showed the officer after the battle how he detected the Indians. The desert sand is normally littered with small tracks made by kangaroo rats, beetles, coyotes, and jackrabbits. Over time these imprints became weathered by wind and rain; however, they can often be seen for weeks. Picayune John knew that it had not rained in quite a spell and the wind had not blown real hard for several days; yet when he inspected the area around the camp several hours after they settled in, there were no tracks at all. Since the Army was camped at Kickapoo springs and it was the only watering hole for many miles, the Indian outriders from the larger group had detected the soldiers and retreated, wiping out their tracks as they moved away, including all the small animal prints. Since the hostile's horses would need water, they would be coming back about dawn with the larger group.

The Seminole-Negro scouts were all Indian in their tracking, endurance, and fighting skills. The young of the clan uttered a mixture of Spanish and Indian. Only the older members spoke English, a holdover from before their escape from slavers and Oklahoma. Since Spanish was the language of the frontier, including the Army officers, these scouts presented less communication barriers than the Lipan and Kickapoo trailers.[27]

The black man's contribution to the settlement of the West has never been fully explored and much has been methodically disregarded. A number of works have been published in recent times documenting the large number of blacks colonizing the Southwest, in particular; but, there is much left to be done. One of the men who early on recognized the capabilities of black cowboys was Charles Goodnight. Bose Ikard was Goodnight's right hand man for many years. Goodnight said that "He was probably the most devoted man to me that I ever had." Ikard even carried Goodnight's money on many cattle drives since Goodnight trusted him and felt that no one would think of the black man carrying the funds. The character Josh Deets, in Larry McMurtry's novel, *Lonesome Dove,* was based on Ikard.

When Ikard died in 1929, he and Goodnight were still good friends. The old scout was buried in Greenwood Cemetery in Weatherford along with Oliver Loving. Goodnight had the following inscription placed on Ikard's tombstone:

> Served with me four years on the
> Goodnight-Loving Trail, never shirked a duty
> or disobeyed an order, rode with me in
> many stampedes, participated in three
> engagements with Comanches, splendid
> behavior. C. Goodnight

Partly because of trouble with local Texans, the band of Seminole-Negroes was relocated in 1874 to Las Moras Creek, about three miles south of Fort Clark. Here the families found better living conditions than at Fort Duncan; however, trouble with the Texans continued.

Fort Clark was established on June 24, 1852 by Major Joseph H. LaMotte with Companies C and E of the First Infantry at Las Moras Spring which provided ample water and had produced a beautiful stand of old oak and pecan trees. By 1874, the Fort housed over 200 men. The Fort served numerous infantry and cavalry units during the Indian Wars of the southwest and more than 12,000 members of the 2nd Cavalry Division, the last horse mounted Cavalry division trained there until deployed overseas in 1944. Shortly after World War II ended, the Fort was closed. The present-day town of Brackettville sprang up near the Fort to provide the commerce that the Fort required.

Trouble for the Seminole-Negro scouts followed them from Fort Duncan to Fort Clark. In December 1874, George Washington, a nephew of Chief John Horse was fatally wounded in the mid-section during a shootout in a Brackettville saloon.

Tensions increased between local ranchers and the Maascogos when the former accused the Black-Seminole community of stealing cattle and horses. In 1876, Chief John Horse and a scout named Titus Payne were ambushed near the Army hospital. Payne died of his wounds and Chief Horse was severely crippled by the attack. Many of the Black-Seminole families packed up and John Horse led an exodus back to Nacimiento. Over the next few years, a number of families gave up on a life in the United States and followed the chief back to Mexico. In 1882, Chief John Horse died in Mexico City shortly after securing papers ensuring the Mascogos rights to their land in Nacimiento.

In early 1877, Adam Payne was killed by a shotgun blast in the back fired by a local deputy sheriff, Calron (Gus) Windus. Payne was shot from so close that the blast caught his clothes on fire.

This is possibly the only case in U. S. history where one Medal of Honor winner killed another. Calron Windus, a native of Wisconsin, won his Medal of Honor as a soldier in the all white 6th Cavalry, at the battle of Little Wichita in Indian Territory in 1870 against the Kiowa. Windus was Bugler and Orderly. His command was surrounded and almost eliminated. Windus and two others volunteered to attempt to break out and seek assistance. They were successful and Windus received the medal for his bravery.

In 1871, he left the military, drifted into Brackettville and was appointed as a Deputy Sheriff of Kinney County. He was engaged to marry Agnes Ballantyne, daughter of James Ballantyne, one of the most prominent men in the County. Windus was on his way up.

Adam Payne (often spelled as Paine in Army records) was born around 1843. As a scout for the Mexican Army, he gained a reputation as an aggressive fighting man, so by the time he arrived in the United States, his aggressive nature was well known. As a Seminole-Negro Scout, he earned his Medal of Honor in September 1874. He demonstrated his ferocity in battle and was given accolades for his skill and bravery. Colonel Mackenzie stated that, "This man has, I believe, more cool daring than any scout I have known."

Payne and two other Seminole-Negro scouts along with two Tonkawas scouts were sent out to search for Kiowas. Suddenly, they were surprised by nearly 40 braves who attacked them without warning. The scouts retreated but Payne provided rear guard action while the others escaped the charge. When Payne's horse was shot from under him, he used it as a breastwork. He killed a Kiowa, absconded with his pony and successfully fled.

Payne did not re-enlist when his service expired in 1875, and he drifted back and forth across the Mexican border. He reportedly stabbed a white soldier in Brownsville on Christmas Eve in 1875. So in December of 1876, he was a wanted man when he ran afoul of Deputy Sheriff Claron Windus.

As Katarina Wittich relates in her article *The Wild West of the Seminole Negro Indian Scouts*, no one really knows exactly what happened on New Years Eve of 1876 but since the shooting of John Horse and Titus Payne, there continued to be unrest in the Black-Seminole community. They were near starvation, they were quarreling among themselves including making threats against each other, and several brawls had occurred, mostly among the Mascogos. While some local white citizens were calling for ousting the scouts and their families, others were requesting that the Army employ more Mascogos as scouts to protect the frontier from bandits and hostile Indians.

Scott Warrior was accused of stealing five horses in August. A few days later, Isaac Payne and Dallas Griner were indicted for the theft of a gelding owned by Deputy Sheriff Claron Windus. These two Seminole-Negro men spent most of the next few months in Nacimiento,

Mexico to avoid the law; yet late December found them back in the Brackettville area to celebrate.

Sheriff Crowell learned that several Mascogos with outstanding warrants would be attending the New Year's celebration at the scout's encampment on Los Moras Creek, possibly at the Zion Baptist Church. The wanted men included Adam Payne, Isaac Payne, and Dallas Griner. The Sheriff, Windus and Jonathan May secreted themselves outside the camp and waited for the opportune time to arrest the outlaws.

Hearing the noisy celebration and dance going on in the village, the officers moved into position. At midnight the families came out of the building and began a shuffling dance around the church. The lawmen stepped from hiding and before anything else happened, Windus fired a double-barreled shotgun at Adam Payne from such a close distance that his clothes were set ablaze.

In the ensuing ruckus of people scattering, screaming, fighting, and shooting, Frank Enoch was mortally wounded. From all accounts, Bobby Kibbett jumped Deputy Windus and wrestled him to the ground. In the smoke and commotion, Isaac Payne and Dallas Griner escaped.

Judge W. W. Arnett was called to the site to perform an inquest. Adam Payne's body was turned over to his family as was Enoch who died a few hours later. Kibbett was charged with attempting to murder Deputy Windus but was later acquitted.

Within a month, Isaac was back from Mexico and re-enlisted in the scouts. Little is known of Bullis' involvement in these troubles but it would be surprising if one were to discover that he did not attempt to help his scouts in these times as he was known to do at other times. Bullis may have entered the affair at this point to get the charges levied by Windus dropped since there were no more incidents concerning those horse stealing indictments.

About this same time, Claron Windus resigned his deputy's position to become the County Assessor of Taxes. He married Agnes

Ballantyne and became a wealthy man. In 1897, his large house became the first house in Brackettville with indoor plumbing. Windus volunteered to re-join the Army during the Spanish-American War and spent a year in Cuba. He died in 1927, a wealthy and successful citizen.

In spite of all the local violence directed at the Seminole-Negro nation, they remained loyal to Bullis and the Army and never strayed from their duty. The Seminole-Negro scouts were finally disbanded in 1914 but the scouting skills were used little after 1881. Many of the early scouts served for many of those years. Issac Payne served off and on until 1901. John Ward served for a total of 24 years before 1895 when he was forced to give up the job because of severe rheumatism. He died in 1911.

Some descendants of the scouts still live in the Brackettville and Del Rio area but many have relocated to other parts of the United States. There are large numbers remaining in Texas and in Oklahoma. In Nacimiento de los Negros today, there are perhaps 350 descendants of the scouts but they are more or less destitute since the waters of the San Juan Sabinas River have dried. Others have drifted to the larger towns and cities of Mexico to survive.

Each third Saturday in September, the descendants return to the Seminole-Negro Scout Cemetery in Brackettville, Texas for a reunion and to remember with pride the valuable service provided by their ancestors in riding the plains of hostile Indians, and to remember their leader and supporter, John Lapham Bullis.

Seminole-Negro Scouts from left are: Unknown, Billy July, Ben July, Denbo Factor, Ben Wilson, John July, and William Shields. Taken at Fort Clark in 1885. (Courtesy Charles G. Downing)

John Jefferson,
Seminole-Negro Scout.
(Courtesy Mrs. John
Jefferson)

Seminole-Negro Scout, Pompei Factor, in later life. Sad to say but he died penniless without government assistance. His fellow scouts paid for his funeral expenses. (Courtesy Wikipedia)

6 ENGAGEMENTS

Bullis and the Seminole scouts saw plenty of action during the years he was in command. Bullis' Service Record lists twenty-seven different times they were in the field in the 97 months since he received the command until June 3, 1881. The length of these details varied from five days to a maximum of six months. The vast majority exceeded two months.

Numerous scouting trips made by Bullis and the Seminole-Negros engaged the Indian. Four of the scouts were awarded Medals of Honor. Three of those received the honor for saving the life of Lieutenant Bullis. Others, judging from extant reports of the conflicts, should have been given consideration for the Nation's highest award, including Bullis himself.

In May 1873, the Kickapoos and Lipan Apaches moved across the U.S. - Mexico border and made a devastating raid on the Texas frontier along the Rio Grande. Colonel Randal S. Mackenzie was ordered to extract revenge for the settlers who lost property and loved ones in the attack.

Mackenzie was a New York veteran of the Civil War, having completed his education at West Point in 1862. He received the brevet rank of Major General of Volunteers by the age of 24. He fought in many battles and established his reputation early as a fighting man. During the war, Mackenzie was brevetted seven times. General Grant once said, "I regard Mackenzie as the most promising young officer in the Army."

Mackenzie was frail as a young man and stood five feet nine inches and weighed about 145 pounds. He was wounded six times in the Civil War and another time during the Indian Wars. It was this arrow wound in the leg that caused him much trouble for the balance of his life.

When the War of the Rebellion ended, Mackenzie reverted to his permanent rank of Captain in the Corps of Engineers. In 1867, he was promoted to Colonel and took command of the black 41st Infantry in Texas. In 1870, he was reassigned to command of the 4th Cavalry on the frontier. In 1883, General Mackenzie was placed in charge of the Department of Texas. He died in New York in 1889 and is buried at West Point.

On the night of the 17th, Mackenzie and six companies of his 4th Cavalry moved out of Fort Clark toward the Mexican border. Earlier reconnaissance by Bullis' scouts had located the hostiles' camps, and it was up to Bullis and the Seminoles to lead the way. Marching all night around obstacles and over difficulties typically found on a march in the darkness through a strange country, Mackenzie's forces encountered the renegades at 7 a.m. on the 18th.

The village, located near Remolia, Mexico, was fifty to sixty lodges strong. It was attacked as soon as the military forces could be shuffled into position. The entire camp, along with its supplies, was destroyed. Nineteen warriors were killed, forty women and children were captured, and the most valuable prize of all, Costillietos, principal chief of the Lipans, was snared. It was reported that the Chief was lassoed by Scout Renty Grayson. Sixty-five ponies were recovered.

Among the captured, a young woman was discovered to be

Costillietos' daughter, Teresita. This woman stayed at Fort Clark and eventually married Black-Seminole Scout James Perryman, possibly in a ceremony officiated by Bullis. She soon proved her worth to the scouts in that she was a very skilled tracker and outdoors woman. Teresita loved to read sign and enjoyed the tracking process enough so that she was often used to assist the scouts in following the trail of marauding renegades.

Mackenzie's losses included three men wounded--one mortally. Bullis and his 16 scouts were commended for their action.

Since the troops had traveled so rapidly, their pack animals had been left behind. The entire command had nothing to eat during the 32 hour dash into Mexico, save what small amount of bread they carried in their shirts.[28]

On an April afternoon in 1875, Bullis nearly lost his scalp. Without the fast thinking and brave actions of his dedicated scouts, Lieutenant Bullis' feats on the Texas frontier would have ended then and there. The lieutenant and three of his best scouts from the 24th, Sergeant John Ward, Trumpeter Isaac Payne, and Trooper Pompey Factor, had just left a small spring in the lower Pecos River country when they crossed a large Comanche trail made by 75 ponies. They followed the tracks in the general direction of Eagle's Nest Crossing on the Pecos. Since the war party was traveling from the settlements and many of the animals were shod and not loaded, the soldiers knew that they had accidentally cut the sign of stolen horses.

After following for about an hour, the scouts tethered their mounts and crept up unobserved on the Indians as the marauders were attempting to cross the river to the west bank. Upon reaching a bush about 75 yards from the dismounted braves, the four troopers opened fire. They kept the heat on with volley after volley for 45 minutes during which time the scouts successfully recovered the horse herd twice only to lose the animals when the Indians tried to circle the small detail. Three Comanches fell and a fourth was wounded by the deadly hail of bullets sent flying their way by the soldiers.

When the braves discovered the meager strength of their attackers, they launched an all out rush on the brush from which Bullis and his scouts were pouring lead. As the Indians were about to outflank Bullis and cut the troopers off from their mounts, the scouts were forced to withdraw.

In the wild excitement that followed, Bullis' horse bolted just as the lieutenant was about to make his getaway. The other three men were already mounted and riding hard when Sergeant Ward looked around for Bullis, who was now turning back to make his last stand against the 25 or so onrushing warriors. Ward called to the other scouts as he wheeled his horse and dashed back to assist his leader. Factor and Payne provided cover fire while John Ward rode by and scooped Bullis from the ground. The return fire from the Winchester-armed Indians filled the air with the smell of cordite and the sound of rifle balls whizzing past. Ward's rifle stock was shattered and the sling was cut by bullets during the miraculous rescue.

Seated behind Sergeant Ward, Bullis and the scouts rode straight through the advancing hostiles, firing as they went. It had been necessary to forget the stolen horses and try to save their own hair. In Bullis' after-action report of the episode, he apologized for losing his horse complete with bridle and saddle, but he acknowledged that his life would have been snuffed out had it not been for the three brave Seminole scouts.

All three of the scouts were awarded the Congressional Medal of Honor for their courageous and soldierly conduct in the rescue of a fellow man. Bullis was commended for his, "energy, gallantry, and good judgement."[29]

The close brush with death did not slow Bullis down. A few months later, he and a Sergeant slipped into an Indian camp under the cover of darkness and *borrowed* nearly thirty horses that had been stolen from settlers.[30]

In July 1875, Bullis and the Seminole scouts along with two companies of the 24th and one company of the 25th were attached to six companies of the Tenth Calvary under the command of Colonel William Rufus Shafter. The huge column of some seven hundred pack mules and a long supply train left Fort Concho in search of hostiles. They covered a large portion of southwest Texas, the panhandle, and a small section of New Mexico Territory over the next four months. The column returned to Fort Duncan on November 15 having killed one brave and captured only five others.[31]

On October 17, Bullis and his Seminoles were on an advance scout for a large force commanded by Colonel Shafter when they encountered a large hostile camp. The Indians had abandoned the camp and fled when Bullis' column approached but they left their bounty. Bullis' command destroyed 25 ponies, fifty sacks of mesquite beans, four thousand pounds of buffalo meat, many buffalo hides, lodge poles, and cooking utensils. If nothing else, this effort likely caused the Indians to experience another hungry and cold winter.

The Seminole Scouts were again on detached service with the forces of Colonel Shafter from April 11 until September 4, 1876.[32] During this long summer, they were almost constantly on the move and engaged in several actions with hostiles.

In June, an incident occurred that gives some insight into the character of Bullis. While in route back to Fort Clark from a scouting detail in the Davis Mountains, Bullis' scouts discovered a fresh Indian trail. The tracks led toward Mexico. Turning onto the tracks, Bullis forded the Rio Grande River about one hundred miles west of the Pecos River junction. This river crossing became known as Bullis' Crossing and is near the tip of the Big Bend Counrty. He searched for three days before the Mescaleros were located. Then naturally, a fight ensued with the Seminole Scouts forcing the Indians to retreat. The scouts collected 36 horses and returned to the American side of the river.

As soon as camp was set up, Bullis dispatched a courier to Fort Clark with a report of the encounter. Since he had chased the band into Mexico, he felt that it was imperative that his commander be made aware of the facts in case the Mexican Government made any noise. After the courier departed, Bullis decided that the report would be better received if he gave it himself.

He instructed the scouts to return to the Fort at the normal pace which a herd of horses could be driven, and he mounted up. Thirty-six hours and one-hundred and forty miles later, Bullis rode up to the main gate of Fort Clark. Alone, he had covered some of the roughest country in Texas in record time merely to deliver in person the report of his encounter with the war party inside a foreign country.[33]

On July 29, Bullis and Lieutenant George Evans of the 10th Cavalry led 20 Seminole Scouts and about 20 Negro troopers into Mexico on the trail of Lipans. They made a dash deep into the foreign soil to roust the hostiles. Twenty-five hours later found them 110 miles away on the bank of the San Antonio River, near Saragossa. Facing them were 23 lodges. In the twilight before sunrise, the soldiers crept up to the sleeping camp and opened fire. At the sound of the first volley, the braces sprang to their feet and charged. Although unorganized, the Indians carried the fight to the Army. It was hand-to-hand and rifle-to-club for the next quarter hour. The detail was almost overrun as the fighting raged all around the perimeter of the camp.

Reports differ as to how many warriors died, but it was between ten and fourteen. Four squaws were captured along with a hundred horses, bearing Texas brands. When the remaining Indians fled, the casualty toll showed that three soldiers had been slightly wounded but none lay dead.[34]

Bullis reduced the village to ashes and began his retreat back to the north side of the Rio Grande, but before the hooves of his mounts got wet, 250 Mexican cavalry soldiers overtook Bullis' command about 30 miles south of the river. It looked desperate since the Mexican commander seemed to have annihilation on his mind. Bullis quickly assumed a defensive position behind natural breastworks and prepared to make his last stand with his 40 men.

Before the shooting started, Lieutenant Colonel William R. Shafter and four companies of United States cavalrymen came into view. There was a lengthy standoff; however, sanity prevailed and the Mexican troops broke off the contact and retired.

Of course, there were official protests that Bullis had raided a Mexican village of peaceful farmers, despite the fact that all the animals recovered wore Texas brands. Major General Edward O. C. Ord issued an order encouraging American troops to pursue marauders into Mexico if the raids continued. In effect, he legitimized and fully supported Bullis' actions.

January 10, 1877, found Bullis and the Seminole Scouts sprinting toward Mexico once again. They had joined up with Captain A. S. B. Keyes and 90 troopers from Fort Clark in pursuit of Kickapoos and Lipans. Deep in the Santa Rosa Mountains, a recently abandoned camp was located and destroyed.

The fall of 1877 was a busy time for Bullis and the scouts. On

September 26, near Saragossa, Mexico, they engaged a fleeing party in a short yet desperate battle. The scouts killed five warriors without losing a single man.[35]

In October, the scouts struck a hostile trail and followed it more than 50 miles into Mexico. They killed five Apache braves and recovered some 60 horses and mules with Texas-registered brands.

In late November, Bullis crossed the Rio Grande with 37 men in pursuit of renegade apaches. The Indians were discovered driving a herd of horses down a deep canyon. It was impossible for the troops to obtain a good field position because when spotted, the Indians climbed to the top of the canyon and had the advantage of high ground. Bullis elected to retire to the American side of the border and live to fight another time.

A few days later, Bullis was accompanied back across the border by the 8th Cavalry under the command of Captain S. B. M. Young. After a long stalk deep into Mexico, the Indians were located near the Carmen Mountains. The 100 plus detachment attacked and succeeded in sending the war party into scattered flight. The hostiles again had the advantage of position which prevented the military from inflicting any great damage but when approached by the large cavalry force, the Indians took no time to gather up any belongings before they escaped. The Army took possession of 17 horses, five mules, one burro, saddles, water kegs 54 deer and buffalo hides, and large quantities of venison and horse meat. They burned everything that could not be carried and returned to Fort Clark by the middle of December.[36]

In early summer of 1878, another incident with the Mexican troops occurred when Captain S. M. Young with a small contingent of cavalry crossed into Mexico in the Devil's River country trailing a band of raiders. Colonel Ranald Mackenzie accompanied Young and only a half day behind, followed Lieutenant Colonel Shafter with 1,500 troopers and a battery of light artillery.

Well into Mexico, Young and Mackenzie encountered some 200 Mexican soldiers. General Valdez told Mackenzie that he intended to stop the American cavalry right there and turn them back to the international boundary. Mackenzie declined the invitation and tempers flared on both sides. The situation worsened and in the afternoon Mackenzie's men, out numbered several times over, moved forward in a skirmish formation.

As tension peaked, the noise of Shafter's large force met the ears of both sides. As the forces came over the hill behind Mackenzie, the Mexican command retired, never to threaten American troops again.

7 EIGHTY DAYS ON AN APACHE TRAIL

During the late fall and early winter of 1878-79, a small party of renegade Apaches from the Mescalero Agency migrated deep into Texas and began raiding outlying settlements and ranches along the Pecos river near its junction with the Rio Grande. These marauders were typical of the bands that were plaguing the Southwest. They moved swiftly and looted at will.

Lieutenant John Bullis was ordered to pursue the hostiles and return them to Fort Clark for trial.[37] He gathered his scouts, a few troopers, some supplies, and on a cold January morning, set out in search of the Apache. What followed were the recorded hardships and sufferings of winter months on the trail, well over 100 years ago.

When Bullis returned, he filed a lengthy and descriptive report of his venture.[38] This report is paraphrased here and documents one of the longest scouting trips in the history of the American Indian Wars. Footnotes have been liberally added in the hope that they will supplement the narrative and close the gap between the writer of yesterday and the reader of today. Many of the quoted phrases are those of John L. Bullis, and his colorful flavor has been retained with the utmost care.

Bullis left from the camp of his Seminole scouts on Las Moras

Creek, near the Rio Grande,[39] on January 31, 1879, about 9 a.m. His patrol consisted of 39 Seminoles and three Lipan Indian scouts;[40] one Mexican packer, Jose Tafoya;[41] two officers, Lieutenant F. D. Sharp, 21st Infantry, and Acting Assistant Surgeon P. C. Gilbert. His total complement was 45 soldiers, scouts, and one civilian packer.

On that first day out, the patrol traveled for about 20 miles to the northwest. They went into camp near the mouth of Sycamore creek about 4 p.m. Bullis almost always noted in his log the camp conditions and many descriptions of the country they passed through. On this date, he noted that the camp contained good grass, wood, and water. He also noted that the night was very cold.

On the second day on the trail, Bullis' party traveled some 18 miles and went into camp at a small post called San Felipe. Shortly after they arrived, Lieutenant Alexander Rodgers, 4th Calvary, and 16 men from companies A and C arrived from Fort Clark and joined the group. Also included in the group from Fort Clark was Acting Assistant Surgeon Eugene McCloon; five wagons with a 10 day supply of forage for the animals; a packtrain containing two-months of rations for the entire force. J. W. Jaycox was the chief packer and he had in his employ 11 private citizens as packers. Bullis' command by now totaled 75 including 59 enlisted men, 12 packers, and four officers.

For the next 8 days, the column traveled generally northwest. On the evening of the 5th day, they camped near old Fort Hudson.[42] On the 6th day, Bullis sent 5 men including Sergeant John Ward[43] up the main road to old Camp Lancaster[44] to deliver mail to the private citizens living there.

On the 11th day out of Fort Clark, the wagons were started back to the fort. During the next day, they were rejoined by Sergeant Ward and his 4 troopers. Ward reported discovery of an Indian trail about 10 days old. He also returned to camp with a broken down pony abandoned by the Indians. Bullis dispatched 1st sergeant David Bowlegs and a few scouts to follow this trail. At dark, they had found 10-12 horses secreted at a small spring about 5 miles west of Bullis' camp. The Indians had not been sighted and had already left the spring.

The next morning, Bullis, a Lipan scout named Far-das-ti and Tafoya left camp and followed the Indian trail west-northwest for about 12 miles. Again, they did not see the Indians and they returned to the camp at about noon.

By now, Bullis was certain he had crossed the trail he was looking for and he broke camp at about 1 p.m. and took to the trail with the entire column. In camp that night, they lit no fires.

Once he cut the sign of the Apache raiding party, Bullis pushed his troops hard in an attempt to overtake the marauders. On the 14th day, the column traveled over "very rough and broken" country for 35 miles. The Lieutenant notes in his log that the stock was in need of water. One of the younger pack mules gave out within sight of the camp. During the night, "he came in."

The following day, the trail took to the main road to Fort Concho[45] for about 6 miles and then broke off to the northwest toward the plains.[46] After 30 miles, the soldiers went into camp near Castle Gap. "A terrible wind came up during the night; men and animals suffered from cold."

The next evening found Bullis and his scouts in camp near Horsehead Crossing on the Pecos River.[47] The next night they camped in the "lower" end of the White Sand Hills[48] "near an old government wagon--it had been abandoned by a surveying party about 1868." Bullis' encampment used the old wagon, some barrels and a few stakes for wood that night. This was the second night out of the last three that they made a dry camp.

The next morning, the need for water was becoming critical so the column moved deep into the sand hills and dug for water without success; moved further into the sand hills and dug again. This time they found "Plenty three to four feet from the surface; quicksand caused the holes to fill up. Men dipped out and watered stock with cups, mess pans, and camp kettles. One pack mule from the train gave out and was abandoned. Fair grass and plenty of willow timber for wood."

On February 18 (19th day out), heavy winds caused shifting sand to obliterate the trail. Bullis ordered the party to continue moving along the line the Indians had been following. After moving some 8 miles to the northeast, Bullis' scouts found where the Indians had dug for water and camped. They also picked up a horse lost or abandoned by the war party. That made both the renegades and the soldiers about even on lost stock because on this same day, Bullis abandoned three young mules along the trail after they gave out. Camp that night was again dry and there was little wood.

On the 20th day, Bullis reported that two of the three pack mules "dropped" the day before they came into camp. The night of the 21st day was another dry camp and Bullis reported losing one pack animal. The 22nd day found the column at Antelope Wells. Bullis reported, "Indians had remained at these wells for about 4 days, but had left the morning before. Found a dead horse in one of the wells; dug it out and watered our animals all day and part of the night. Good grass and very little wood."

Now the raiding party had rested up and was moving out rapidly. Bullis pushed his party as hard as he dared for the next few days. His column was covering nearly 30 miles a day. He crossed into New Mexico Territory about 25 miles south of the mouth of Seven Rivers.

Bullis and his party were now in Lincoln County which covered the entire southeast corner of the Territory. The County was larger than the state of Ohio and at that time had less than 2,000 residents, mostly of Mexican decent. The County seat was in the village of Lincoln, located along the Rio Bonito.

Flames of the famous Lincoln County War were still smoldering when Bullis and his party entered the county. Life, indeed, held little value for some since so many had died in the fighting that had consumed the residents for more than a year. Billy the Kid, Jessie Evans, John Selman and other gunmen still roamed the countryside. This was a desolate and forbidding land where the price of a cow was often a life and gunplay ran rampant.

The soldiers camped the next night at the foot of the Guadalupe Mountains at a spring where the hostiles had camped the night before. Bullis reports that, "Five young pack mules from the train gave out this day. Packers and scouts succeeded getting them into camp by midnight."

On Feburary 25th (26th day out), Bullis indicated that he had pushed some of the trailing party too hard in a vain attempt to capture the hostiles. "Young pack animals in train much worn, so much so, that I concluded to send 12 mules and a number of ponies belonging to the scouts into Fort Stockton, Texas, 200 miles distant, thinking to save the animals. Detailed three Seminole and two Lipan scouts and one citizen packer. I put Private Joe Corn in charge, the instructions to take his time; these animals all reached Stockton and were saved. Had they continued with the command on the trail, all would have been abandoned."

Fort Stockton was established at Comanche Springs, a strategic water source along the Great Comanche War trail in 1858. Its first mission was to protect travelers on the San Antonio--El Paso road which used the spring as a watering hole. The location of the Fort is in the current town of Fort Stockton, on Spring Street between Second and Fifth Streets. The Post was decommissioned by the Army in 1886 once the hostile Indian threat was abated.

On this same day, the scouting party crossed a large Indian trail and found an abandoned camp site. This party of Indians had about 100 horses and a woman and child with them. Bullis believed that they were then camped near his troops in the Guadalupe Mountains. Bullis stuck to his original trail and continued to pursue the Indians that had raided back along the Rio Grande River in Texas.

On the 27th day, the Lieutenant reported that he had been three days without water for the animals. The stock would not eat, and he lost one pack mule during the march that day. During the night, two pack mules broke loose and ran away. He also notes that the men are suffering for water as well.

The next day, thankfully, the soldiers found water about 2 p.m. and spent the rest of the day and all night watering animals. He notes that they gave each animal "about three quarts."

Bullis had been pushing hard but he was sure that he was gaining on the hostiles. He had lost many animals and those remaining with the detail were suffering greatly, as were the men. From his post-scout report, it is clear that John Lapham Bullis was concerned about the men and animals. It is also apparent that he intended to locate and capture the hostiles just as his orders stated.

Suddenly, on February 28th (29th day out) about mid-morning, "One Lipan and one Seminole ran under the cover of a bluff toward me and reported horses and they thought Indians just in front of us. I had the men close up and tighten their saddle girths thinking we were near them at last. We worked around undercover of the hills and trees for about half an hour expecting to see an Indian camp at any moment. Found that the Indians had left eleven horses and had continued west-northwest. I sent parties out hunting water. David Bowlegs, 1st Sergeant Seminole scouts reported a small spring . . . with water sufficient to fill forty canteens."

At this point, the need for water was again acute. Bullis split his forces and sent Lieutenant Rogers with a detail and the pack train back to the location of the previous night's camp. Bullis and his scouts went to work cleaning out the seeping spring discovered by Bowlegs. His report stated that, "I was fearful of losing all of my animals from want of water: they suffered terribly during the day."

Within an hour, they had "water boiling up to such an extent that three animals drinking could not lower it . . . Very many of the large mules and horses drank 10 buckets each." Rogers was recalled since Sergeant Bowlegs' discovery contained enough water for the entire column. Bullis named the location "Salvation Spring."

At dark that evening, the Lieutenant mustered the scouts for pay. It is amusing that on the last day of the month, no matter where the Army was or how remote they were from the nearest commercial facility in which to buy a drink of whisky, the United States Army paid its wages just the same.

Bullis and his detail remained in camp at the spring for the next three days, resting the men and animals. He sent two scouts back to look for the two mules that broke loose from the pack train three nights before. On the third day, the scouts returned with the two wayward mules.[49] During this entire time, Bullis had lookouts posted on the highest mountains around camp.

On the 33rd day, they dropped one old pack mule and camped with no water for the animals. The next night, they camped along the Rio Penasco about 60 miles from Fort Stanton and about 30 miles from the Mescalero Indian Agency.[50] Bullis also reports that, "Several ranches are at this point and the citizens reported that the Indians had passed five days before. The Indians had killed one of their work oxen as they passed. Five citizens had followed them to the Agency, and the Agent caused the Indians to give the owner of the ox two of the horses that the Indians had brought in as payment. When questioned by the Agent (Mr. Godfroy) as to why they had killed the ox, the Indians said that they had been on a long journey (which we are well aware) and were hungry. I purchased forage for the animals."[51]

Bullis and his trackers trailed the Indians to "within three miles of the Agent's (Mr. Godfroy's) house." Godfrey promised Bullis that he would try and get the Indians to turn the hostiles over to the Army.

As farther evidence that this was an unsettled country, on Government issue day at the Agency for the Indians, August 5, 1878, the soil turned blood-red over events that should have never happened. There were crowds of Indians around the Agency that day receiving their rations handed out by the Government. Women and children milled around the headquarters while Indian horses grazed along the Tularosa River. As had often happened in the past, local horse thieves would rush in and grab a few horses while the Indian owners were busy with receiving their rations. The Indians had learned to post guards with the horses just in case.

Near mid-afternoon, the guards who were some distance from some of the animals spotted a group of riders on a nearby hill. Convinced that the cowboys were after the horses, the guards yelled and rushed toward their charges. Chief Clerk of the Agency Morris J. Bernstein dropped his pencil at the tally book and grabbed a nearby horse and galloped after the guards. With Bernstein in the lead, the sentinels went over the hill and out of sight.

Rifle and pistol reports came to the ears of those still at the headquarters area. When the smoke cleared and Agent Godfroy arrived at the scene, he saw one Indian on the ground and his clerk riddled with bullets. As a ball whizzed past his head, Godfroy retreated and sprinted for support of a detachment of Fort Stanton soldiers who were camped about a mile away. The soldiers galloped to the location only to see the invaders withdrawing.

Who were the raiders? Billy the Kid and his faction of the Lincoln County War were blamed for the incident but no one was ever charged with the murders and there is scant evidence that the Kid actually pulled the trigger. This was just another incident that occurred during the War.

On April 4, 1878, only a few miles west of the Agency at Blazer's Mill, Andrew L. (Buckshot) Roberts found himself surrounded by members of the opposite side of the conflict, including Billy the Kid. Buckshot was alone and he faced eleven of the enemy. Meeting face to face, Charles Bowdre shot Roberts in the midsection with the first round. Roberts fired his rifle and hit Bowdre on his belt buckle, knocking him to the ground. The slug glanced off the buckle and hit George Coe on his trigger finger, removing the last joint.

Shooting now became general. Roberts backed into Dr. Blazer's office and fell to the floor, firing as he went. As the Kid's group scrambled for protection, John Middleton was hit, although not seriously. Dick Brewer hid behind a wood pile as did several others. When he raised up to fire at Roberts, he was shot clean through his head and was dead when his body reached the dirt. The killing of Brewer took the fight out of the attackers and they fled to tend their wounded. Brewer was beyond help but the other three Roberts had hit needed medical attention.

Roberts lingered until the next day when he died about noon. Less than 24 hours after Brewer was buried, Roberts was placed beside him.

Civil strife became so serious that the United States Government dispatched Frank Warner Angel, an independent attorney from New York City to investigate the troubles and report back to Washington. Angel was in Lincoln County and taking testimony from mid-May until late June of 1878. He submitted a lengthy report in early September resulting in the New Mexico Territorial Governor Samuel B. Axtell being replaced by Lew Wallace of the novel *Ben Hur* fame. Thomas Catron, United States District Attorney for the Territory also resigned in October of 1878.

In a separate report filed with the Bureau of Indian Affairs,

Record Group 75, National Archives, entitled "The Examination of Charges Against C. F. Godfroy," Angel charged the Agent with mishandling of Government funds and property. As a result, Godfroy submitted his regination in late September; however, since there was not an available agent to replace him, Godfroy stayed on until a replacement could be located and sent to the Territory.

These illustrations serve to underscore the condition of the unrest in Lincoln County at the time Bullis arrived. It is of little surprise that Agent Godfroy seemed less than interested in going to any length to assist soldiers from a distant fort in Texas looking for stray Apaches.

On the 39th day from Fort Clark, Bullis and his worn band of troops arrived at Fort Stanton, New Mexico Territory. Along the trail that last day, Bullis' detail met General Edward Hatch, 9th Cavalry, Commanding District of New Mexico. Hatch was on his way to Santa Fe and was to pass by the agency. The General said he would discuss the matter with Godfroy.

General Hatch sent Bullis a letter dated that same day, March 10, 1879. This letter is contained as attachment "A" in the report:

> My dear Lieutenant:
>
> The Agent Major Godfroy, is anxious to give you every assistance in securing the Indians trailed to the Reservation. It may not be in his power to secure them himself, but is perfectly willing that you should secure them yourself. They are not Indians who come in regularly for rations; they are called coyotes by the reservation Indians. We call them dog Indians; they belong to some band struck by Captain Carroll last summer. The Captain

may be able to give you more information and he is familiar with the country.

I think the Indians should be secured and taken with you on your return. You can talk with the Agent freely. He is ready to give you all the assistance in his power.

Yours truly,

(signed) Edward Hatch[52]

For the next week, Bullis and his command camped near Fort Stanton and rested both men and animals.

Fort Stanton, founded in 1855, is located in Lincoln County, New Mexico on a high plateau five miles from the present day town of Capitan. It is in this area that the first Smoky the Bear was rescued from a forest fire. The Fort enjoys cool weather in the summer and mild winters with some snowfall.

The Fort was home to Colonel "Kit" Carson and his New Mexico Volunteers from 1862 to 1864. During this time, Carson placed Mescaleros and Navajos on the Bosque Redondo Reservation but the experiment was not wholly successful and many Indians jumped the reservation. In later years, the Fort provided military support for the nearby Mescalero reservation. It was abandoned by the Army in 1896. The site is currently used by several state agencies.

On the fifth day in camp, Bullis heard that a new Agent had passed by to relieve Godfroy. Captain Carroll and Bullis hurried down the trail to over take the new Agent. They discussed the matter with him and he stated he would write Bullis the following day concerning the hostile Indians.

On the seventh day in camp, the following letter arrived for the Lieutenant. This letter is contained in Bullis' report as Attachment "B:"

> Lieutenant Bullis,
>
> Sir:
>
> Major Godfroy assures me that there is no probability of the Indians you mentioned to me coming in--or to use his own language--"you might as well look for a needle in a hay-stack," as to try to get them.
>
> Respectfully,
>
> (signed) S. A. Russell[53]

Agent S. A. Russell was in the process of replacing current Agent Godfroy. As cited before, Special Agent Frank Warner Angel working for the Department of the Interior had concluded an investigation against Major Frederick C. Godfroy. It was found that he probably had been involved, before the start of and during the infamous Lincoln County War, in padding the books on deliveries made to the Indian Agency, accepting bug-infested flour, and illegally disposing of government property. The testimony was so conflicting that no criminal charges were pressed and he was allowed to resign.

Disappointed, the scouting party left camp the next morning and started down the long trail back to Texas.[54] The detachment moved down the Hondo River Valley to its juncture with the Pecos River. They generally followed the Pecos River to the vicinity of Fort Clark, ensuring a good source of water on the way home.

This failure to capture the renegade Apaches was not at all unusual. For more times than not, the Army simply could not contain the hostile Indians on the run; a small band of warriors moved faster and knew the lay of the country better.

Bullis' unsuccessful attempt to extract the renegades from the reservation near Fort Stanton was not the only incident involving this Agency. Lieutenant McMartin trailed a raiding party to the Mescalero Reservation in August of 1879. He too was refused assistance by the agent. After two confrontations in four months, the Department of the Interior issued orders to the Indian Agent that every effort would be made to aid troops in rounding up hostiles. The guilty ones were to be turned over to the proper authorities for punishment. Of course, a letter did no good, and McMartin also returned empty handed.

Bullis and his detail marched on wearily toward their home post. Each evening, they camped after marching anywhere from 13 to 29 miles. On the trip home, they enjoyed good grass, wood, and water, thanks to the Pecos River and the springtime when the grass started growing again.

About 8 a.m., on the 52nd day out of Fort Clark (March 23rd), a courier caught up with the column carrying a dispatch. This telegram directed Bullis to remain at Fort Stanton to await further instructions by order of Lt. Col. William Shafer, Adjutant, 24th Infantry.

Bullis states in his report, "As my men and animals were terrible worn, I thought I would be justified in not turning back to Stanton." He marched on toward Fort Clark.[55]

The detail crossed to the east side of the Pecos River at Pope's Crossing. They continued on down the river day after weary day. On April 1, 1879 (61st day),[56] they arrived at Fort Stockton and camped on the creek near the post.[57] The "Men sent in with worn-out animals from the Guadalupe Mountains, New Mexico, reported with the animals in fair condition."[58]

Bullis remained at Fort Stockton for three days and then resumed his journey. On the night of the 70th day, Bullis reported that, "A fire ran us from camp about 3 a.m. It leaped the river and made such rapid progress that we barely saved our equipment. One mule was burned severely about the head, but was saved by the exertions of Corporal William Jennisson, Company "A", 4th Cavalry."[59]

On the 74th day,[60] "Had a mule bitten by a snake and had to abandon it."[61] The next day, at Pecan Springs, Bullis received a letter from the Commanding Officer at Fort Stanton directing him to return to that post. Bullis states, "From the condition of my animals, I felt justified in joining my station at Fort Clark, distant about 80 miles."

This letter had been sent from Captain George A. Purington, 9th Cavalry to Lieutenant G. W. Smith stationed at Roswell, New Mexico and apparently mailed to Pecan Springs in order to intercept Bullis and his men. It was dated March 24, 1879. It only took 21 days to catch up to Bullis and his men.[62]

On the 80th day (April 19), the command reached Fort Clark. Bullis reports: Men and animals much worn from hard service. Total distance marched, 1266 1/2 miles. Officers and men endured the hardships and privations incident to such an expedition remarkably well.

I would here state that the stock found by us on the Indian trail was completely used up, being footsore, and so worn out as to be unable to travel, and that I divided the animals among my best scouts, subject to the approval of higher authority.

They were subsequently abandoned or traded by the scouts on the return trip to Texas with one exception. One mare was claimed by a citizen at Fort Stockton, and being convinced that his claim was good the animal was turned over to him.

Bullis signed his 28-legal-sized page, and hand-written report with the salutation: "I am very respectfully your obedient servant, John L. Bullis, 1st Lieut., 24th Infantry, Commanding Scouting Expedition."

Lieutenant Bullis' report passed through many hands before

finally arriving at the Department of the Interior in Washington. It was endorsed by Colonel Ranald S. Mackenzie, Commanding the Headquarters District of Nueces, Fort Clark, Texas. It was then forwarded to the Adjutant General, Military Division of Missouri, by Brigadier General E. O. C. Ord, Commanding the Department of Texas. Lieutenant General P. H. Sheridan, Commanding the Division of Missouri, sent the documents to the Adjutant General of the Army in Washington. On July 10th, 1879, Bullis' report was transferred from the War Department to the Department of the Interior, in whose National Archives files it rests today.

As Bullis stated above, the officers, men and even the animals endured a daunting trek of 1266 miles and 80-days across a parched, barren, dun-colored, mesquite and creosote bush dotted wasteland. About all the life they saw were jack rabbits, sage brush, and other desert-dwelling critters. They wore out several sets of horseshoes as well as the animals that wore them. It was a grueling expedition that testifies to the hardships suffered by the Black soldiers and their white officers in the years required to contain the threat of the native Indians and convert West Texas to a safe land for settlers and their families.

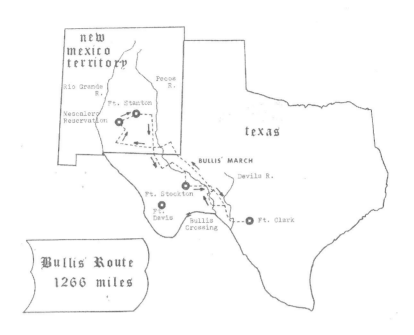

Bullis' route in 1879 while trailing Apache Indians into New Mexico Territory and return. (Author's map)

8 LAST BATTLE

The Apache Chief, Victorio, and his band of renegades raided in the United States almost at will, and when pursued, fled to Mexico. Then some time later, the hostiles would again return north of the border and kill and steal for a few days before the soldiers could catch up to them and flee across the border once again. Finally, the Army had enough and commenced an important mission along the Texas border with Mexico involving the 9th and 10th Cavalry along with the 24th Infantry.

Detachments of soldiers manned waterholes, river crossings, and other vital locations in the vast wasteland. By denying the Apache leader life-sustaining water and the opportunity to slip into the United States undetected, the renegades were forced to remain in Mexico. In the late summer of 1880, Victorio was surrounded and killed by Mexican troops. The great leader's death pretty much signaled the end of organized and large-scale Indian trouble in Texas.

This campaign shows the endurance of the black soldiers. West Texas is a harsh environment in the summer yet the Negro soldiers had the stamina to hold out for the many months it took for Victorio to be run to ground. It was a hot, dry, windy, demanding, and lonely duty, but the black troopers persisted long enough to be successful.

In their last important encounter with hostile Indians, Bullis and his scouts once again displayed their incredible tracking ability. By 1881, the Indians had given up on Texas and had ceded it to the white man. Only occasionally did a drunken brave or two cause any trouble. For the most part, the Indians were miles away. Reservations elsewhere held them outside the boundaries of the Lone Star State. This last conflict by the scouts is credited by many historians as being the last action with hostile Indians in the state. Bullis' scouts literally brought an end to the Indian wars in Texas.

On April 14th, a small party of liquored up Lipans attacked the home of Mrs. McLauren near the head of the Frio River. They killed the woman and a young lad named Allen Reiss, stole everything of value, and fled.

Twelve days lapsed before the pursuit order was handed down, but the scouts took to the trail under instructions from General Stanley to "pursue and destroy."

The Indians killed a horse before leaving the McLauren place, and wrapped the hoofs of their mounts in the hide so the animals would leave less distinctive tracks. It is amazing that the scouts were able to even locate a two-week old trail made by horses wearing booties, let alone follow it. The faint tracks may be the reason they took Perryman's wife Teresita with them on this pursuit.

But follow it they did; over the rugged, rocky, and arroyo-laden country along Devils River. The tracks crossed the Rio Grande some ten miles below the mouth of the Pecos. Somewhere along the way, Teresita discovered, probably from reading the evidence left by the passing warparty, that the renegades were from her tribe. She attempted to quit the scout then and there. Concerned that her goal was either to warn the Lipans or to mislead the scouts, she was not allowed to leave.

From existing accounts, she was tied to her saddle and there she stayed until the troops returned to Fort Clark.

Bullis camped on the American side at dark on the 30th. Crossing into Mexico at first light the following morning, the scouts stalked the raiding party into the Sierra del Burro Mountains.

At 4 p.m. on May 2, a scout spotted the hostiles' camp lying in "a rough and broken country." He immediately reported to Lieutenant Bullis that the braves were bedding down about two miles away. Bullis concealed his party until about midnight when he took twenty-seven scouts and crept toward the camp. Seven scouts were left in charge of the detail's horses with instructions to be ready for flight if anything unexpected developed.

The Indians never suspected that they would be followed after so many days had elapsed and they had traveled so many miles into Mexico. What they did not know was that their back trail was covered by "The Whirlwind" and his Seminoles. It has been said that "only an Indian can catch an Indian" and with Bullis and his thirty-four Seminole-Negro scouts on their trail, the hostiles were up against thirty-five "Indians."

At daybreak, the scouts exploded from hiding like a swarm of angry bees. Four bucks and a squaw were killed. A boy and a wounded squaw were captured as well as twenty-one animals. The scouts, as usual, suffered no casualties. The captured woman and boy spent the balance of their days on the reservation.

Bullis' Service Record indicates that a sub-chief of the Lipans named San-da-ve was mortally wounded in this fight. It was later learned from Mexicans that the chief died a few days after the battle.[63]

As far as Texas was concerned, the Indian was gone. In 1881, Army patrols covered nearly 4,000 miles, but no Indian sign was found after April.[64] The black troops in Texas had taken away the hostiles ability to obtain water and move about undetected. They had destroyed the Indian's sanctuaries on the Staked Plains and in Mexico. The renegades had no place to go except the reservations or the unsettled country of Mexico's Sierra Madre Mountains where some held out for a few more years, rarely venturing north of the border.

The absence of hostiles to track brought an end to the need for scouts. Their numbers slowly decreased as the Seminoles were released from the Army and sent home to tend their flocks and raise vegetable gardens. Finally, in 1914, the order was issued to dissolve the remaining complement of Fort Clark scouts.

The loyal Seminole-Negro scouts never received the land that was promised once their military service was complete. A number of these heroes of the American frontier died as paupers, never even receiving a pension from the United States government as even a slight acknowledgement of their service to the Nation.

Pompey Factor, Congressional Medal of Honor winner for saving Bullis' life in 1875, died penniless in 1928. He still carried the empty box in which the medal had arrived. He was denied a pension for the last time in 1926 but was told the Army had no records of his service. His $86.40 funeral expenses were paid by a friend. He is buried in the Seminole Indian Scouts Cemetery in Brackettville, along with the other three Medal of Honor recipients.

Bullis, however, received numerous citations for his service in ridding the frontier of marauding Indians. Several of these awards came shortly after his affair with the Lipans in the Burro Mountains.

In 1881, he was presented with a beautifully engraved sword by the people of Kinney County as a token of their undying gratitude. That same year another ceremonial sword was received and was inscribed, "Presented to Jno. L. Bullis by the people of West Texas. He has protected our homes - our homes are open to him."65

On April 7, 1882, he was honored by a joint resolution adopted by the Texas House of Representatives and the Senate. The commendation reads:

> Resolved by the House of Representatives, the Senate concurring, That we tender our sincere thanks in the name of the people of this State, to Lieutenant J. L. Bullis, of the Twenty-fourth Infantry, United States Army, for the gallant and efficient services rendered by him and his command in behalf of the people of the frontier of this State, in expelling the depredations of Indians and other enemies of the frontier of Texas.66

Also in April, a letter to the President of the United States:

Forty-seventh Congress Committee on Military Affairs, House of Representatives, Washington, D. C., April 14, 1882

> To the President,
>
> In view of the long and distinguished military services rendered by Lieutenant John L. Bullis, on the frontier of Texas, for which our people are very grateful, we cheerfully commend him to favorable consideration for promotion...No officer of the grade of Lieutenant Bullis stands higher in Texas.67

Colonel Shafter complimented the Lieutenant saying, "He has been a zealous, faithful officer, and his success in overtaking and punishing marauding Indians has been remarkable. He has rarely failed to recapture stolen stock and punish parties that he had been in pursuit of."[68] Brigadier General D. S. Stanley said, "There is no officer now in the Army with such a record."[69]

Company I, 25th Infantry in dress uniform at Fort Snelling, Minnesota in the late 1880's. (Courtesy national archives: U. S. Signal Corps photo)

Detachment of 24th Infantry in Deer Russell, Wyoming, 1898. (Courtesy National Archives: U.S. Signal Corps photo)

9 BULLIS LEAVES TEXAS

After thirteen years and eleven months on the Texas frontier, Bullis left his beloved Seminole-Negro Indian Scouts under the command of others and followed the Twenty-fourth into Indian Territory (now Oklahoma) in the latter part of 1881, and assumed his post at Fort Supply. Here, his command was merely watching over the more peaceful reservation Indians. It must have been dull duty for a former Indian slayer.[70] Other units of the 24th were stationed at Forts Reno and Sill.

This camp was established by Lieutenant Colonels Alfred Sully and George A. Custer on November 18, 1868 near the junction of Wolf Creek and the North Canadian River as a forward base for General Sheridan's campaign of 1868-69. Four days later, Custer won the battle of the Washita and retuned to Camp Supply with his captives.

In 1878, the Camp was re-named a Fort of the same name and was manned until 1895. The site is now an Oklahoma State hospital.

The camp's solitude was once described by Colonel Joseph H. Potter, Commanding Officer of the twenty-fourth in these words:

> The distance from . . . [Fort Supply] to Fort Reno is one hundred and

twenty miles, to Fort Elliott, Texas is ninety-two miles, to Dodge City, Kansas is seventy-four miles.

Most of Bullis' duties consisted of watching over and keeping the reservation Indians of the Territory on the reservation while at the same time preventing white interlopers from invading the reservation. The troops also performed fatigue and other required garrison duties as well as a large variety of construction details. One company was ordered to cut and trim a thousand poles for the construction of a telegraph line between Fort Supply and Fort Dodge. They were in the field for two weeks. Another company was assigned to install the line and was in the field for two months.

About the only distraction for off-duty soldiers stationed at Fort Supply came from the post sutler since the post was remote from any civilian town. This trader was allowed to sell food, drink, and light wine, but he was forbidden by law to sell hard liquor to the troops. He also maintained a billiards room for entertainment of the soldiers.[71]

All-in-all, being stationed in the Indian Territory was ever bit as bleak as the Texas assignments and there was little trouble with the reservation Indians to provide any break from the routine monotony. There were not the far ranging scouts as there had been on the Texas frontier since the more peaceful Indians of the Territory tended to remain on the reservations.

There was a white man by the name of Payne that provided the Army with much grief. He continued his bad habit of promoting white settlers advancing on reservation land for several years. Since the penalty for violating the reservation boundaries was only a small fine, if anything, Payne organized forays onto Indian lands time and time again. The Army would then have to forcibly remove the farmers from the reservation. There is little doubt that this was a distasteful duty for the soldiers since this caused a major disruption to the poor sodbusters and their families.

About the only benefits acquired by the relocation to Indian Territory was some improvement in the weather since Oklahoma received more rainfall than most of west Texas and the accommodations. Fort Sill, for example, had stone barracks with heated bathing facilities. The large disadvantage was the remoteness from civilian towns.

On November 24, 1884, Bullis was granted a four month absence because of sickness. The Assistant Surgeon stated in the report that Bullis was suffering from chronic malarial poisoning and chronic rheumatism, and had been for the past two years. This is the only indication in Bullis' file that he had ever reported for sick call.[72]

After four and a half years, the 24th Infantry was relocated to New Mexico Territory for a few months, and a much deserved promotion for Bullis to the rank of Captain.

In June 1888, the 24th Infantry moved to the Department of Arizona. Bullis became the Acting Indian Agent at the San Carlos Apache Reservation. He had now become the Government manager of the Indians who, only a few years before, he had been stalking to the death. For the next six years, he listened to the problems of his wards. There can be little doubt that Bullis made a good Agent, but it is almost certain that he felt a sadness for the wild and free Apache he had once chased; now remanded to captivity.

Garrisons of the 24th occupied the reservation as well as Forts Grant and Apache. The post accommodations in Arizona were about the worst the 24th had ever had to endure. There were no bath facilities when they arrived and the Fort buildings were in major disrepair. Again the extreme remoteness of the frontier caused much boredom for the troops. Nevertheless, the infantry command preformed their duties with little desertion.

The troops were relieved from the boredom and extreme heat by marksmanship training and other activities including education. They were also heavily engaged in construction of adequate facilities for themselves. By the time the command left

Arizona, they had constructed gymnasiums, bowling alleys, and canteens. The troops produced theater productions and debating teams, not to mention the basic housing facilities such as barracks and mess halls.

The weather at San Carlos was somewhat like that on the Texas frontier except that the heat was worse. It could reach 110 degrees on a cool day. The country was barren and was graced with little rainfall. The duty at San Carlos was so rough that the troops were exchanged every six months with soldiers from the garrison.

Frederic Remington tells in his writings of a visit to the San Carlos Reservation during the time that Bullis was the Agent. According to Remington, the reservation was a vast tract of desert and mountains through which ran the Gila River. On a great flat plain near the river stood the long, low adobe buildings and lines of white tents to house the troops. Remington stated, "San Carlos is a hotter place than I ever intend to visit again."

Remington's intention was to paint the natives. Bullis told him with a twinkle in his eyes, "Young man, if you desire to wear a long, gray beard you must make away with the idea that you are in Venice." Remington related that the Apache might be coaxed into standing still for a photograph but not long enough for a painting.

It was ration issue day for the Indians and almost everyone on the reservation was at the headquarters to receive the Government's handout of flour, beef, and other staples. Remington relates:

> The day was very hot, and we retired to the shade of Captain's Bullis' office. He sat there with a big sombrero pulled to cover his eyes and listened to the complaints of the Indians against one another. He relegated certain offenders to the guard house, granted absolute

divorces, and probated wills with a bewildering rapidity.

By evening, the Indians were gone; gone back into the hills and valleys to await the next issue day. Bullis was then left with the dull chores of his normal duties as Indian Agent.[73]

In his report for 1890, Bullis reported that of the seventeen renegades still including Massai and the Apache Kid, 15 had either been killed or captured by the military. The Kid and Massai were still at large and had made several raids on the reservation, killed several married women and kidnapped several girls. These two had terrorized good Indians and attempted to persuade unhappy braves to follow them on the hostile trail.

The Apache Kid and Massai evaded all Bullis' efforts to contain them and they were still active long after Bullis had moved to greener pastures in New Mexico Territory. These two renegades got away from Bullis.

From all indications, the Kid was dead about five years after Bullis left the San Carlos position. The Kid occasionally visited his sister, Mrs. Argo Watson, on the San Carlos reservation and she said that she never saw him after 1896.

Massai, on the other hand, continued looting, killing and living in the wild with a family consisting of a wife and five children until he was dispatched by cowboys in the Black Range Mountains in the fall of 1906.

In order to prevent an uprising, in March of 1890, Bullis caused 75 men, women and children who were relatives or sympathizers of the renegades to be sent to Mount Vernon Barracks in Alabama where many former renegade Apaches, including Geronimo and Naiche, were being held after they were transferred from Fort Marion, Florida.

One of those interned was Eskiminzin who petitioned for release in 1892. At that time, Bullis wrote that,

"I would say that he was arrested at my request, as he was a disturbing and dangerous element on the reservation. At the time of his arrest, I had positive proof that he had rendered assistance to renegade Indians [some 16 of them], all of whom were murderers, and who evaded the military authorities by hiding in the mountains of old Mexico and Arizona and some of whom have not yet been captured (Apache Kid and Massai). Eskiminzin aided them by furnishing them with food and ammunition. As to his self support, for several years he lived off the White Mountain Reservation [south of it, on the San Pedro River] where his many crimes caused the people to rise up in arms against him and he for self protection, fled to the Agency, where he and his entire family lived for years supported by the Government Ration. . .Since his removal comparative peace has reigned on the reservation."

Through the efforts of Bullis and others, Eskiminzin remained in captivity for many years.

On July 2, 1886, a black Baptist Chaplain had joined the 24th Infantry. Chaplain Allen Allensworth was an ex-slave who had served in the Union Navy during the Civil War. He was educated at Roger Williams University in Nashville, Tennessee and had taught at one of the freedmen's Bureau schools.

Allensworth's application for the regimental chaplain position of the 24th was endorsed by his former owner, Mrs. A. P. Starbird. He was appointed by President Cleveland in the spring of 1886. Since the chaplain was charged with providing at least an elementary education of the soldiers, Allensworth served as school master for the members of the unit. The Chaplain became know throughout the Army as a fine educator and his curriculum became the standard for the military. This man was a Godsend to the illiterate members of the 24th and other regiments by providing an education and Christian doctrine that served them well in the Army and contributed to their becoming fine and productive citizens once their enlistment expired.

Without doubt, Bullis was in favor of educating the black soldiers and supported Allensworth in his efforts. Bullis held a great deal of affection for his black comrades-in-arms and always wish for them a better life. When the famous Chief of Scouts in Arizona, Al Sieber, made the following statement in the *Arizona Citizen* issue of September 25, 1889 in answer to a question about why conditions at San Carlos produced so much unrest among the reservation Indians, John Bullis became upset and the strife between the two strong-willed men set the stage for conflict.

> First and worst of all, is the Negro soldiers that are stationed at the post. They are a disturbing element, and beyond control, or rather are not controlled. Their presence is a menace to the peace of the reservation, and a disgrace to the government that keeps them there. They put in their time hanging around the Indian squaws and bucks. They will procure any thing that an Indian wants and has the money to pay for, whiskey, ammunition, and other things which the reservation rules forbid them having. . .

Over time, Sieber feelings intensified and his criticism of the Army and the Agent became more vocal. Tension between the two intensified. Sieber seemed to think that Bullis' treatment of the Apaches was unjust. Both men had hunted Apaches for many years but while Bullis' fondness seemed to lie with the blacks, Sieber's defiantly was with the Indians.

Dan Thrapp in his book *Al Sieber, Chief of Scouts* cites a letter he received from Bud Ming in 1958 that provides some additional insight into the character of Bullis:

> The last time I saw captain Bullis was October, 1889. I was with my father and other ranchers delivering a bunch of steers to butcher for the Indians. We corralled the steers at sundown in the big adobe corrals, camped there for the night. Next morning at daybreak Bullis was there. They went to weighing out the steers on the Government scales . . . Bullis was turning gray at this time, rather short, not tall, his face inclined to be full, not sharp, nice features, pleasant, and friendly, will liked by all--Indians, whites, civilians, a friend of the ranchers adjoining the reservation. He had all kinds and classes of people to deal with. San Carlos was of the Territory. Military personnel from Fort Huachuca, Fort Bowie, Fort Grant, Fort Thomas came that route moving to other posts to the north. San Carlos was the junction of the wagon road to Fort Apache on White River, going east and north to Utah and Colorado. Bullis was prominent and known by all. He operated mining claims at Tully Springs, 20 miles south from San Carlos and 3 miles from the old Aravaipa Post Office. He did not put in any time there but kept men at work.

Ming's statement of "well liked by all," did not include Sieber and his cohorts. According to Frank C. Lockwood, Bullis was using his Apache charges without compensation to build an elaborate system of roads on the reservation and construction of other improvements. To keep the Indians under control and working on the Agent's plans for improvements to San Carlos, Bullis kept the guardhouse full of Apaches whether charged or not. The fear instilled by this treatment kept the Indians working on improvement projects but infuriated Sieber.

Finally, the pot boiled over and Sieber, who had spent twenty years of his life scouting for the Army and working with the Apaches, had been permanently crippled by a bullet fired by one of his Apache scouts, and had become a rheumatoid afflicted old man, told Bullis straight to his face what he thought of him. Bullis acted quickly and tossed Sieber off the reservation with very short notice.

Shortly after Sieber was dismissed, an article in the T*ombstone Prospector* reported that "Captain Bullis is a man of means and is considered to be worth a half million dollars made by fortunate investments in Texas lands." The verbal feud continued.

In November 1890, Bullis closed the Indian trader's store owned by Ezra W. Kingsbury who was a 60-year old Civil War veteran. The Agent's reasons for his actions stem from a case of liquor that arrived at the store addressed to one of the black soldiers. Bullis instructed the storekeeper to hold the box until the soldier came to pick it up and he would be arrested in possession of the contraband by a scout Bullis assigned to watch the store.

A clerk in the store took instructions from the soldier in question through a 3rd party to ship the container to Globe. In Kingsbury's absence this was done and Bullis accused the trader of conspiring to protect the guilty party so he ordered the trader's business closed.

This event eventually caused two different investigations to be conducted at the Reservation by the order of the Commissioner of Indian Affairs. Charges and counter charges flew back and forth between the Agent and the cranky Kingsbury. The trader accused Bullis of having an affair with his housekeeper, mistreating the Indians, frustrating an investigation into the alleged molestation of a small girl, among many other things.

Bullis defended himself very well and the investigation reports complimented the Agent for attempting to disrupt the delivery onto the reservation of the liquor indicated that it was all because of a misunderstanding by the clerk when he forwarded the case of liquor to Globe. Bullis was ordered to re-open the trader's store which exasperated him greatly and he fired off more letters attempting to defend his position.

Although Sieber appears to have been nothing but a bystander in this entire affair, some of Bullis' correspondence implicates the Chief Scout. Was Bullis simply taking advantage of the situation to rid himself of a thorn or was Sieber actually involved? Possibly. The Chief Scout was a known card player at the table of Kingsbury but that association would hardly justify making him the fall guy in the entire episode. To read the sorted details of the event, see *Al Sieber, Chief of Scouts* by Thrapp.

Citizens of the area polarized in their support of either Bullis or Sieber and numerous newspaper articles and discussions of right or wrong ensued. The net result of the hard feelings, verbal skirmishing, and investigations was that Bullis was cleared of all accusations, Kingsbury was allowed to re-open his trading store, and Al Sieber, without fanfare, went off up the road toward Globe, Arizona Territory kicking rocks. In a letter dated February 2, 1891, Sieber wrote that "I have nothing more to do with the Indians and am clade (Sic) of it."

The old scout might have been better off if he had continued to have nothing more to do with Indians but that was not to be. In later years, long after Bullis had moved on, Sieber once again became associated with the Apaches. He took to running work gangs made up of Apache Indians. They were building the Tonto Road on Feburary 19, 1907, when a large rock they were trying to dislodge could not be moved. The old scout called for a work stoppage while he hobbled on his painful arthritic joints and .45-70 damaged leg down the slope under the boulder to see what could be done. As Sieber peered under the several ton monster, the boulder shifted and fell, apparently by its own volition, and smashed the life from the aged scout. Sieber died as he had lived – fearlessly and in the presence of his Apaches.

Did the Indians kill their leader of days gone by? Perhaps. There will always be speculation. Certainly he had some enemies among the renegade Apaches that he chased and killed for so many years, but he also defended them in later years and was well respected by those that served as his Apache scouts.

February 27, 1890, brought Bullis his long awaited rewards for the gallant action on the Texas frontier. He was brevetted a Captain and a Major on the same day. The testimony given in his behalf provides insight into the feelings the frontier people had for the "Thunderbolt."[74]

Congressman Thomas M. Paschal said Bullis, ". . .has won a place in the confidence, respect, and admiration of the entire people of the State of Texas, that has never been surpassed and but seldom equaled in the history of this State...his...name is especially dear to the people of Texas."[75]

Major F. S. Dodge stated, "I know of no one who, by reason of hard and hazardous service on the frontier and in the field is entitled to more consideration."[76]

The Governor of Texas, Edward J. Davis, related, "I feel a great interest in the future of...John L. Bullis."[77]

Bullis served as Agent for San Carlos until November 24, 1891, when he was succeeded by another military man, Lewis Johnson.

The Government authorities apparently pointed no blame toward Bullis because of the Sieber and Kingsbury scandals because after leaving San Carlos the Captain relocated east to New Mexico territory to serve as Agent for the Pueblo and Jicarilla Indians. His headquarters was in Santa Fe, where he arrived in 1893.[78]

In the fall of 1896, the 24th Infantry Regiment was transferred to Fort Douglas on the northern outskirts of Salt Lake City. For the first time in the unit's long history, the entire Regiment was brought together at the same location and they were billeted near a major city. It was like a reward long overdue the black soldiers for their many years of hardship in the remote Southwest. Their fight to open the American frontier was over and they were given a short respite before being dispatched to Cuba during the Spanish-American War where they were to accompany Teddy Roosevelt on the charge up San Juan Hill.

On January 29, 1897, Bullis was promoted to Major and appointed U. S. Army Paymaster.[79] He served in this position for several years. Major Bullis was continuing in his military role as a desk jockey. His days of action were over.

The paymaster filed an Individual Service Report in San Francisco, California on June 30, 1902, while he was awaiting transportation to Manila, Philippine Islands for occupation duty that was required for many years after the Philippine Insurrection was officially ended by President Theodore Roosevelt on July 4, 1902. The unrest continued until 1913 and at the peak of occupation, there were 70,000 American troops on duty.

Bullis stated in the Individual Service Report that he was married and had three minor children;[80] that as paymaster, he had been "almost constantly employed in the payment of troops and other accounts;" that he spoke and could translate Spanish; that he was versed in the "management of the wild tribes of American Indians or similar people;" and that he had been an Army officer for almost forty years.[81]

Mandatory retirement age caught up with Bullis in 1905. But, before being put out to pasture, the military bestowed upon him a richly deserved reward. He was promoted to the rank of Brigadier General on April 13, and he left the Army for good on April 14, 1905.[82]

Bullis decided to return to his adopted and beloved Texas when his career ended. He settled in San Antonio, close to his old stomping ground, and built a handsome home at 621 Pierce Avenue on the corner of Pierce and Grayson Street.[83] Here he enjoyed reliving the bygone days with old friends – both white and Indian alike.[84] Even in his winter years, the General craved action. He was a great fan of the prize fight game, and it was while attending a bout that the ex-scout fought his last battle; on May 25, 1911, General John Lapham Bullis suffered a stroke and died.[85] His 70th birthday was celebrated less than a month before

John Lapham Bullis. (Courtesy *Army Navy Courier*)

Bullis' retirement home, Pierce Avenue and Grayson Street in San Antonio. This structure is located across the street from Fort Sam Houston and is now known as The Bullis House, a Bed and Breakfast. (Author's Photo)

Bullis Gap looking generally to the southeast toward Mexico and the Rio Grande River. This pass is in the Bullis Gap Range of mountains about 25 miles southwest of Sanderson, Texas. (Courtesy Shane Jahn)

Looking Southeast toward Mexico from the southwest side of Bullis Gap. The mountains in the far background are across the Rio Grande River and are in Mexico. (Courtesy Shane Jahn)

Camp Bullis established in 1917 as a training base for Fort Sam Houston. The camp once occupied 12,000 acres northwest of San Antonio, Texas. (Courtesy Internet)

Camp Bullis barracks with tents in background. Probably taken during WWI. (Courtesy Internet)

FOOTNOTES

1. Joseph Peters, *Indian Battles and Skirmishes on the American Frontier*, 6.

2. *Ibid.*, 6.

3. *Ibid.*, 11-12.

4. *Ibid.*, 12.

5. *Ibid.*, 13.

6. *Ibid.*, 10.

7. Dorman H. Winfrey and James Day, *The Indian Papers of Texas and the Southwest* 1825-1916, 450.

8. Peters, *op. cit.*

9. Winfrey and Day, *op. cit.*, 419.

10. Cordia Sloan Duke and Joe B. Frantz, *Six Thousand Miles of Fence*, 3-7. This story of the famed XIT ranch was written by Mrs. Duke who was the wife of the last General Manager of the huge spread. She recalled many of the anecdotes from her life on the range. Others were obtained from the cowboys that had worked the empire. It is an interesting book describing the early Texas cattle days.

11. John Trebbel, *The Compact History of the Indian Wars*, 193.

12. Lieutenant Frederick E. Phelps, " Phelps: A Soldiers Memoirs," *New Mexico Historical Review*, XXV, January 1950, 203.

13. John M. Carroll, *The Black Military Experience in the American West*, 211.

14. Carlysle G. Raht, *The Romance of Davis Mountains and Big Bend Country*; Phelps, *op. cit.*, 214.

15. Raht, *op. cit.*

16. Carroll, *op. cit.*, 210.

17. *Ibid.*, 207 and 210.

18. Frost Woodhull, "The Seminole Indian Scouts on the Border." *Frontier Times*, December, 1937.

19. Statement as to the Military Record in the United States Army of Brevet Major John L. Bullis, 24th Infantry, U. S. Army, Military files, National Archives, Washington, D.C.

20. *Ibid.*

21. *Ibid.*

22. Edward S. Wallace, "General John Lapham Bullis, the Thunderbolt of the Texas Frontier, I", *Southwestern Historical Quarterly*, Vol. LIV, April, 1951, 452-457.

23. *Ibid.*, 460-461.

24. Service Record, *op. cit.*

25. Carroll, *op. cit.*, 156.

26. Service Record, *op. cit.*; William H. Leckie, *The Buffalo Soldiers*, 97-98.

27. Carroll, *op. cit.*, 203-215; William Loren Katz, *Black Indians: A hidden Heritage*,76-88; Thomas W. Dunlay, *Wolves for the Blue Soldiers*, 105. Archie Waters, "Black Seminoles Carried Day as Scouts in Early America," *El Paso Times*, November 24, 2000.

28. Service Record, *op. cit.*; Peters, *op. cit.*, 35. When the troops left the fort, they did not know where they were headed until they crossed the Rio Grande into Mexico. Invading a foreign country without permission was an open act of war; however, the U.S. War Department looked the other way--the sanctuary that the Indians had been using as a base camp for raids into the States had to be broken. The troops marched 160 miles in 32 hours. Bullis was promoted to First Lieutenant on June 20, 1873, shortly after the raid into Mexico.

29. Service Record, *op. cit.*; Carroll, *op. cit.*, 207 & 266; Swisher, *op. cit.* Scout Adam Payne (his name was misspelled in the nomination letter from General Mackenzie as Paine) received the Medal of Honor in 1874 for action in Palo Duro Canyon. This made Payne the first African-American-Seminole to be so honored. Adam Payne was a cousin to Isaac Payne.

30. Carroll, *op. cit.*,210.

31. Leckie, *op. cit.*, 143-146. William Shafter was an officer in the Michigan Volunteers during the Civil War. He applied for a regular commission at the close of the conflict, and as a lieutenant colonel of the 24th Infantry, he commanded Fort Davis in the early 1870's. As a major general of volunteers, he led them in Cuba during the war with Spain. Shafter retired in 1901. His death occurred in 1906. Bullis and Shafter were also business partners in the Presidio Mining Company, Shafter, Texas. The four original owners of the company were General Shafter, Lieutenant Bullis, Lieutenant Wilhelme, and the man who discovered the strike, John Spencer. The mine was located in the Texas Big Bend country. Over time, Bullis became a major landowner in the area. Even the Texas Supreme Court got into the act over a land title between Bullis

THE WHIRLWIND

and his partners in the Presidio Mining Company. The high court heard cases in 1887 and 1889 concerning land ownership. In this same area was a small seep known as Bullis Springs and referred to by former buffalo hunter Frank Collinson in his book entitled *Life in the Saddle*, page 206. In addition to Bullis Springs and Bullis Crossing, other places in Texas carried his name. There is Bullis Gap Ridge in the Bullis Gap Range of Mountains in eastern Brewster County about twelve miles west of the Rio Grande and some 25 miles southwest of present-day Sanderson, Texas. The highest peak in the ten mile long range is 3,073 feet. There was a non-agency station on the Southern Pacific Railroad in southeastern Val Verde County known as Bullis Station. The original name of the location was Seminole but after Bullis defeated a party of Indians who were camped there, the name was changed when the station was constructed in honor of the victorious commander. A village known as Bullis sprang up around the station but when the station was abandoned in 1944, the village slowly vanished. It is also reported by Robert Wooster, *Soldiers, Sutlers, and Settlers*, 208, that while Bullis was stationed in West Texas, he acquired more than 53,000 acres in Pecos County alone.

32. Service Record, *op. cit.*

33. Raht, *op. cit.*, 205-208; Edward S. Wallace, "General John Lapham Bullis, Thunderbolt of the Texas Frontier, II," *Southwestern Historical Quarterly*, Vol. LV, July, 1951, 82. Permission to enter Mexico when in hot pursuit of Indians on June 1, 1877.

34. Peters, *op. cit.*, Part I, page 59 & Part II, page 39; Carroll, *op. cit.*, 211.

35. Lechie, *op cit.*, 152; Carroll, *op. cit.*, 211.

36. Carl Coke Rister, *The Southwest Frontier* 1865-1881, 187; Phelps, *op. cit.* 213; Carroll, *op. cit.*, 213.

37. Bullis' Report is filed in the National Archives, Record Group 75, Bureau of Indian Affairs, Letters Received from New Mexico 1879, location W-1544.

38. Bullis filed his report with Lieutenant Joseph H. Dorst who was the Acting Assistant Adjutant General of the District of the Nueces, Department of Texas from October, 1878 until October 1879.

39. At the time of this detail, the Seminole scouts were living on Las Moras Creek about three miles from Fort Clark.

40. The Lipans belonged to the Apache family and were originally from the Texas Big Bend country.

41. Jose Pieda Tafoya, a half-breed Mexican and Tonkawa Indian, had accompanied Colonel Ranald S. Mackenzie at the famous battle of Palo Duro Canyon in September of 1874. Because of his activities as a scout for the Army, it is reported that Quanah Parker stated that, "If he ever laid eyes on Tafoya, he would broil him in the fire." Tafoya had previously been involved in the Comanchero trade.

42. Fort Hudson was established in 1857 on Devil's River at the south side of the big bend where the river turns east. It was here that the Army conducted some of its experiments with camels in the desert. The Fort was abandoned in 1868.

43. Sergeant John Ward was one of the three scouts who received the Medal of Honor for saving Bullis' life in 1875.

44. Camp Lancaster, 1855-1861, was located on the Pecos River at Live Oak Creek east of Fort Stockton. The Fort was briefly re-occupied after the Civil War but finally became a ghost post by 1874.

45. Fort Concho was located at San Angelo, some one hundred miles east of Bullis' location. Concho was another camp established in 1867 to protect the frontier. It was left to the elements in 1889. In 1930, a group of citizens acquired the site

to house the West Texas Museum. Today it is renamed the Fort Concho Museum

46. Here the hostile Indians had separated, with the main party continuing and three turning back toward the settled area of the frontier.

47. Horsehead crossing of the Pecos was a favorite ford during the trail driving days, and was located southwest of the present-day site of Crane, Texas.

48. The sand hills of which Bullis speaks are located near the present town of Monahans.

49. This is another example of the tracking ability of the Seminoles. Very few people today could hope to find two animals in an endless country when the trail was three days old. Bullis was looking out for the government property or he would have just reported the mules lost. Salvation Spring is located at the north end of the Guadalupe Mountains in Chaves County, New Mexico. The spring is 18 miles south of the village of Dunken and was later named Bullis Spring. The spring is in Bullis Canyon. Bullis Lake is located less than two miles southwest of the spring. In the present day these locations are all surrounded by the Lincoln National Forest. Ms. Beth Mahill of Mayhill, New Mexico told the author that her great-grandfather, Claiborne Gentry Prude, owned what is now Bullis Spring Ranch. This ranch was in the Prude family for at least four generations. Prude and his brother, Buck came to New Mexico Territory in 1888 and first settled in the community of Weed. Claiborne Prude was born in Fayetteville County, Texas on January 9, 1855. In 1897, Claiborne Prude acquired the Bullis Spring Ranch. There was and is ample water from Bullis Spring to support his cattle operation and family. As he moved west, Claiborne Prude was in the Brady, Texas area before moving on and stopping for several years in the Fort Davis, Texas area. When he moved on west, his brother, John stayed behind in the Davis Mountains and founded the famous Prude Ranch near Fort Davis. Claiborne Prude died on May 2, 1940 in Artesia, NM. This was still

rugged and unsettled country when the Prude family acquired the ranch and without doubt, there were still roaming bands of Apaches, although no longer hostiles, passing through the area on hunting expeditions and watering at the spring as they had for a thousand years. Prude's settlement at Bullis Spring in 1897 was only nineteen years or so after Bullis trailed hostile Indians past the same spring.

50. The Mescalero Agency (also known in those days as South Fork) Headquarters of today is at Mescalero, New Mexico. In 1879, the headquarters was at Blazer's Mill, a few miles west, being named for Doctor Blazer who operated the mill.

51. When Bullis talks of forage, he is referring to grain. The animals were, of course, grazing on native grasses during the trip, but Army thoroughbred horses were normally grain fed and a trip in unsettled country where grain was not available took its toll.

52. Edward Hatch was an officer of the Iowa Volunteer Cavalry during the Civil War. He received, in 1867, brevets of brigadier and major general for gallantry at the Battles of Franklin and Nashville in 1864. He was a colonel of the 9th Cavalry from its organization in 1866 until his death in 1899.

53. Agent S. A. Russell served at several Reservations including Abique before coming to Mescalero. He sported a long white beard and shortly after Bullis' encounter with him Chief Victorio apparently riled at the Agent, grabbed Russell's beard and flung him around and around the room. All the time, Russell crying for the interpreter, Jose Carillo to "talk pretty" to the enraged Chief. The confrontation did not end until the Agent had been pushed from his office. Russell immediately wired Fort Station for help with unruly Indians. The presence of the troops settled things down temporarily. On August 21, 1879, Agent Russell notified Fort Stanton that Victorio and his band left the Reservation. Victorio was destined never to return. He raided all along the western side of New Mexico before moving into Mexico where he was killed by Federales.

54. When this letter arrived, Bullis gave up on being able to return the Indians to Texas and started for home, six hundred miles away.

55. There is no indication in Bullis' Service Record that his superiors disagreed with his decision to ignore the order to return to Fort Stanton.

56. Either Bullis was running low on cash or he just failed to mention that he paid the troops off on the last day of the month.

57. It is interesting to note that during the entire scout, Bullis and his men camped out even when near an Army post. Apparently Bullis did not leave his men under the stars while he slept in a bed when at Fort Stanton or Fort Stockton. He seemed to really feel that what was good enough for his men was good enough for him.

58. These were the men under command of Private Joe Corn who left the main detail on February 25th in the Guadalupe Mountains and took twelve mules and a number of ponies to the fort.

59. A wildfire on the plains has always been dreaded. A fire driven by a strong wind can move at an incredible speed and consume everything in its path.

60. In his report Bullis dropped a day. The dates are correct but he skipped the 71st day.

61. It was not just wild Indians that made soldiering tough, even the wild beasts were against them.

62. Maybe a courier had taken the dispatch literally, "overtake him at Seven Rivers or beyond." If so, the messenger had trailed Bullis for about four hundred miles.

63. Rister. *op. cit.*, 267-268; Service Record; Carroll, 214; Edward Wallace, "General John Lapham Bullis, Thunderbolt of the Texas Frontier, II," *Southwestern Historical Quarterly*, Vol. LV, July, 1951, 83. Teresita died that same year, 1881,

from unknown circumstances. It causes one to wonder if the treatment she received on the scout contributed to her demise. She reportedly left two sons with the Perryman name.

64. Carroll, *op. cit.*, 214.

65. Service Record. *op. cit.*; Edward Wallace, "General John Lapham Bullis, Thunderbolt of the Texas Frontier, II", *Southwestern Historical Quarterly*, Vol. LV, July 1951, 84. These swords have been on display at the Whitte Museum, San Antonio, Texas.

66. Service Record, *op. cit.*; Frank Oppel, *Frederic Remington, Selected Writings*, 117-119.

67. *Ibid.* It was another two years before Bullis received the promotion recommended in the letter to the President.

68. *Ibid.*

69. *Ibid.*

70.. *Ibid.*

71. Fowler, *op. cit.*, 74-78.

72. Service Record, *op. cit.*

72. *Ibid.* Frank Oppel, *Frederic Remington, Selected Writings*, 117-119.

74. *Ibid.*

75. *Ibid.*

76. *Ibid.*

77. *Ibid.*

78. Edward Wallace, "General John Lapham Bullis, Thunderbolt of the Texas Frontier, II", *Southwestern Historical Quarterly*, Vol. LV, July 1951, 84.

79. Service Record, *op. cit.* The 24th Infantry went on to serve gallantly in the charge up San Juan Hill during the Spanish-American War in 1898. They served in the Philippine Insurrection until 1902. During the Mexican Punitive Expedition in 1916, the 24th was under the command of Brigadier General John J. Pershing and invaded Mexico searching in vain for the Mexican guerrilla Pancho Villa.

80. Bullis had not spent all of his time on the trail of Indians. He had married Alice Rodriguez of San Antonio in 1872, but she died in 1887. In 1891, he married another San Antonio lass, Josephine Withers. Three daughters were born to this union.

81. Service Record, *op. cit.*

82. Ibid.

83. San Antonio Express, August 7, 1934. The beautiful structure is now a well advertised Bed and Breakfast, by the name of "The Bullis House."

84. It has been reported that when Colonel William F. "Buffalo Bill" Cody brought his Wild West Show to San Antonio, General Bullis was his guest. Bullis visited with the old warriors traveling with the show and renewed old acquaintances. Bullis could call almost every one of the Indians by name.

85. Posthumously, Bullis was awarded another honor with the establishment of Camp Bullis in 1917 as a target range and maneuver camp for training soldiers during the First World War. The camp was located fifteen miles northwest of San Antonio, between the Fredericksburg and Blanco roads. After the war, the camp was used for demobilization. By 1940, the Army had built permanent facilities at the camp. In 1931, a ten-bed infirmary, an officers' mess, a post exchange, a landing field and other improvements had been built. In 1926 two films were made on camp Bullis - *The Rough Riders* depicting the famous charge up San Juan Hill and the 1927 Academy

Award-winning *Wings*. Several Government Agencies used the camp in the 20's and 30's including the Civilian Conservation Corps and several military units. During the Second World War, the 2nd, 88th, and 95th Infantry Divisions trained at the camp. After the war, one-half million soldiers were mustered out of the service at the facilities. The camp has been used almost continuously in a number of activities since the war and has served as a training base for every conflict since its establishment. The 28,000 acre camp is under the jurisdiction of Fort Sam Houston in San Antonio, Texas. Between 1941 and 1944, over 1,000 troops training at Camp Bullis went on sickcall with concurrent fever, rash, adenopathy, and cytopenia. In each case, the physical examination detected numerous tick bites, suggesting an arthropod-borne infection. The syndrome, coined "Bullis fever," was short lived, but convalescence was protracted. Investigations implicated the Lone Star tick (Amblyomma americanum) as vector. The end of the war heralded a sharp decline in the number of troops training at the Camp and also brought an abrupt end to the disease bearing its name. The clinical specimens collected during the epidemic no longer exist. Increased insecticide use, drought, and predation have decimated the region's tick population. Seven decades after the epidemic, Bullis fever seems fated to remain enigmatic.

BIBLIOGRAPHY

BOOKS AND ARTICLES:

Ball, Eve. *In the Days of Victorio*. University of Arizona Press, Tucson, 1970.

Ball, Larry D., *The United States Marshals, of New Mexico and Arizona Territories, 1846-1912*, University of New Mexico Press, Albuquerque, 1978.

Burton, Art T., *Black, Buckskin, and Blue*, Eakin Press, Austin, 1999.

Carroll, John M. *The Black Military Experience in the American West*. Liveright Publishing Co., New York, 1971.

Clum, Woodworth. *Apache Agent, The Story of John P. Clum*. Hougton Mifflin, Boston, New York, 1936.

Collinson, Frank. *Life in the Saddle*. Edited by Mary W. Clarke, University of Oklahoma Press, Norman, 1963.

Cozzens, Samuel Woodworth. *Explorations & Adventures in Arizona & New Mexico*. Castle, Secaucus, 1988.

Custer, Elizabeth B., *Boots and Saddles*, University of Oklahoma, Norman, 1961

Dale, Edward Everett. *The Indians of the Southwest*. University of Oklahoma Press, Norman, 1949.

Duke, Cordia Sloan and Joe B. Frantz. *Six Thousand Miles of Fence*. University of Texas Press, Austin, 1961.

Dunlay, Thomas W. *Wolves for the Blue Soldiers*. University of Nebraska Press, Lincoln and London, 1982.

Eckhardt, C. F., "The Whirlwind, Lt. John Lapham Bullis and the Seminole Negro Scouts", Internet Source

Ferris, Robert G. Series Editor. *Soldier and Brave*, United States Department of the Interior, National Park Service, Volume XII, Washington, 1971.

Florin, Lambert. *New Mexico and Texas Ghost Towns*. Superior Publishing Co., Seattle, 1971.

Fowler, Arlen L. *The Black Infantry in the West, 1869-1891*. University of Oklahoma Press, Norman, 1996.

Gwaltney, William. "Footprints Along the Border." Fort Laramie National Historic Site, Fort Laramie, Wyoming. Written by Mr. Gwaltney when he was stationed at Fort Davis National Historic Site. Internet Source.

Katz, William Loren. *Black Indians: A Hidden Heritage*. Atheneum, MacMillan Publishing Company, New York, 1986.

Kirkpatrick, Linda. "Teresita, Woman of the Apache." Internet Source.

Leckie, William H. *The Buffalo Soldiers*. University of Oklahoma Press, Norman, 1967.

Littlefield, Daniel F. *Africans and Seminoles: From Removal to*

Emancipation. Greenwood Press, Westport, Connecticut, 2001.

Lockwood, Frank C. *The Apache Indians*. Macmillan Company, New York, 1938.

Mayhall, Mildred P. *Indian Wars of Texas*. Texian Press, Waco, 1965.

McCright, Grady E. and Powell, James H. Disorder in Lincoln County." Rio Grande History , Number 12, New Mexico State University, Las Cruces, 1981.

_____. *Jessie Evans: Lincoln County Badman*, Creative Publishing Company, College Station, 1983.

McCright, Grady E. "John Bullis: Chief Scout." *True West*, Vol. 28, No. 9, Iola, Wisconsin, October 1981.

_____. "Lincoln County Hysteria." *Rio Grande History Number 9*, New Mexico State University, Las Cruces, 1978

Mulroy, Kevin. *Freedom on the Border: The Seminole Maroons in Florida, the Indian Territory, Coahuila, and Texas.* Texas A & M Press, College Station, 1993.

The Online Handbook of Texas. Internet Source.

Oppel, Frank, compiled by. Frederic Remington, *Selected Writings*. Castle, Secaucus, 1981.

Otero County Pioneer Family Histories, Volume 1. Tularosa Basin Historical Society, Alamogordo, New Mexico 1981.

Otero County Pioneer Family Histories, Volume 2. Tularosa Basin Historical Society, Alamogordo, New Mexico 1985.

Peters, Joseph. *Indian Battles and Skirmishes on the American Frontier*, 1790-1898. Argonaut Press LTD., New York, 1966.

Phelps, Lieutenant Frederick E. "Phelps: A Soldiers Memoirs." *New

Mexico Historical Review. XXV, January, 1950.

Raht, Carlysle Graham. *The Romance of the Davis Mountains and Big Bend Country.* The Rahtbooks Company, Odessa, 1963.

Rickey, Don, Jr. *Forty Miles a Day on Beans and Hay.* University of Oklahoma Press, Norman, 1963.

Rister, Carl Coke. *The Southwestern Frontier - 1865-1881.* The Arthur H. Clark Company, Cleveland, 1928.

Robinson, Sherry. *Apache Voices, Their Stories of Survival as Told to Eve Ball.* University of New Mexico Press, Albuquerque, 2000.

Stiles, T. J., "Buffalo Soldiers," *Smithsonian*, p. 82, December 1998.

Swisher, Kevin. "Frontier Heros," *Texas Highways*, Vol. 39, No. 7, July 1992.

Terrell, Alex W., *Cases Argued and Decided Before the Texas Supreme Court, 1887,* Google Internet Source, pp. 581-591.

Thrapp, Dan L. *Al Sieber, Chief of Scouts.* University of Oklahoma Press, Norman, 1995

Trebbel, John. *The Compact History of the Indian Wars.* Hawthorn Books, Inc., New York, 1966.

Trimble, Marshall. *Arizona.* Doubleday & Company, New York, 1977.

Utley, Robert M. *Fort Davis.* National Park Service Historical Handbook Series, No. 38, 1965.

Walker, A. S. Sr., *Cases Argued and Decided Before the Texas Supreme Court, 1889,* Google Internet Source, pp.540-556.

Wallace, Edward S. "Border Warrior." *American Heritage Magazine,* Volume 9, Issue 4, June 1958.

_____. "General John Lapham Bullis, The Thunderbolt of the Texas Frontier, I." *Southwestern Historical Quarterly*, Vol. LIV, April 1951.

_____. "General John Lapham Bullis, The Thunderbolt of the Texas Frontier, II." Southwestern Historical Quarterly, Vol. LV, July, 1951.

Webb, Walter Prescott. *The Handbook of Texas*, Vol. 1, The Texas State Historical Association, Austin, 1952.

Winfrey, Dorman H. and James M. Day. *The Indian Papers of Texas and the Southwest 1825-1916*. Pemberton Press, Austin, 1966.

Wittich, Katarina. "The Mascogos." LWF Communications, Trotwood, Ohio, 2002. Internet Source.

_____. "The Wild West of the Seminole Negro Indian Scouts (or The Killing of Adam Paine, Medal of Honor Winner.)." LWF Communications, Trotwood, Ohio, 2000. Internet Source.

Woodhall, Frost. "The Seminole Indian Scouts on the Border." *Frontier Times*,

Vol. 15, No. 3, December, 1937.

Wooster, Robert. *Soldiers, Sutlers, and Settlers*. Texas A & M University Press, College Station, 1987.

NEWSPAPERS:

San Antonio Express

Waters, Archie. "Black Seminoles Carried Day as Scouts in Early America," *El Paso Times,* November 24, 2000.

Johnson, Cecil. "Goodnight's Top Hand Was One of Few Black Cowboys in History Books," *Las Cruces Sun-News*, February 4, 1995. Reprinted from article in *Fort Worth Star-Telegram*.

MAPS:

Perry G. Van Arsdale, "Pioneer Texas Map."

Texas and New Mexico Highway Maps

Dove Mountain, Texas—Coahuila, U. S. Geological Survey map of 1985

DOCUMENTS:

Fort Davis document provided by the Fort Davis National Historic Site, National Park Service, Department of the Interior

General Orders No. 10, Headquarters Department of Texas, San Antonio, May 12, 1875. Typescript obtained from James Fenton.

National Archives, Washington, D. C.

Statement as to the Military Record in the United States Army of Brevet Major John L. Bullis, 24th Infantry, U. S. Army.

John L. Bullis, Report of Scout, Record Group 75, Bureau of Indian Affairs, Letters Received from New Mexico Territory, 1879, Location W-1544.

Muster Rolls, Seminole-Negro Indian Scouts. Researched and compiled by Bennie J. McRae, Jr. Internet Source.

The 24th Infantry Regiment and the Racial Debate in the U. S. Army. Willard S. Squire III, Maj. USA, Master's Thesis, University of Tennessee, Knoxville, 1985.

INTERVIEWS:

Robert Baca, Monument Manager, Fort Selden, October 2, 1976.

James Fenton via phone, December 13 and December 30, 1976.

James Fenton in Las Cruces, New Mexico, March 23, 1977.

Beth Mahill in Mayhill, New Mexico, Several interviews from 2007-2011.

LETTERS TO AUTHOR:

Vera M. Bullis, December 29, 1976; January 23, 1977.

Kent Carter, Federal Archives and Records Center, July 12, 1976.

Claudia J. Eckstein, Witte Memorial Museum, October 20; November 1, 1976.

James I. Fenton, March 29; April 8, 1977.

Jerry L. Kearns, Library of Congress, November 23, 1976.

Richard S. Maxwell, National Archives, February 13, 1976.

Military Photographs, National Archives, July 28; December 18, 1976.

Military Service Records, National Archives, July 23, 1976.

Judy Ranney, Institute of Texas Cultures, January 21; February 8, 1977.

Judy Robinson, *San Antonio Express and News*, February 10; February 17, 1977.

John L. Slonaker, Military Historian, Carlisle Barracks, December 30, 1976.

Colonel William Strobridge, Military Historian, Washington, D. C.

ABOUT THE AUTHOR

Grady E. McCright arrived in New Mexico from Texas in 1966. He was immediately enamored with both the country and the history. In 1983, he and co-author James H. Powell published *Jessie Evans, Lincoln County Badman*, Creative Publishing Company, College Station, Texas.

Over the years, McCright has written and published 6 additional books of western fiction and western-historical fiction under both his own name and the pen name of Ira Compton. All of these fiction books are available in paper and Kindle format from Amazon. In addition, he has written another non-fiction concerning the Lincoln County War entitled *Cause and Effect* in Kindle format. After a more than 32 year career with the National Aeronautics and Space Administration (NASA), McCright and his wife Marie retired to Cloudcroft, New Mexico in 1998

Other Books by Grady E. McCright

Jessie Evans, Lincoln County Bad Man, by Grady E. McCright and James H. Powell, Creative Publishing Company, College Station, Texas, 1983

*A Stranger Rides In, by Ira Compton (Pen Name), Western Fiction,1997

*Paco, The Apache Tracker, by Ira Compton (Pen Name), Historical Fiction, 1997

*Widow's Plight, by Ira Compton (Pen Name), Western Fiction, 2000.

*The Salt War, Unrest in El Paso, by Ira Compton (Pen Name), Historical Fiction, 2000.

*Sign of Passage, Punitive Expedition into Mexico after Pancho Villa in 1916, by Grady E. McCright, Historical Fiction, 2008

*Massai: The Last Apache Outlaw, by Grady E. McCright, Historical Fiction, 2008

*Cause and Effect, by Grady E, McCright, Non-fiction on Lincoln County and Frank Warner Angel's Report, 2012.

NOTE: All are available from Amazon.com.

*Kindle format as well as paperback

Made in the USA
Middletown, DE
31 August 2016